THE
CROSS-COUNTRY SKI TECHNIQUE BOOK

THE CROSS-COUNTRY SKI TECHNIQUE BOOK

BY BOB WOODWARD

Leisure Press
New York

A publication of Leisure Press.
597 Fifth Avenue, New York, N.Y. 10017
Copyright © 1983 by Leisure Press
All rights reserved. Printed in the U.S.A.

No part of this publication may be reproduced
or transmitted in any form or by any means
electronic or mechanical, including photocopying, recording,
or any information storage and retrieval system now known
or to be invented, without permission in writing from the publisher,
except by a reviewer who wishes to quote brief passages
in connection with a written review for
inclusion in a magazine, newspaper, or broadcast.

IBSN 0-88011-123-2
Library of Congress Number 82-83918

Cover design by Tanya Edgar

TABLE OF CONTENTS

Foreword

Part I: Basic Cross-Country Techniques

    Chapter 1: To the Tracks............................11
    Chapter 2: The Diagonal Stride....................15
    Chapter 3: First Movement with Poles............31
    Chapter 4: Adding the Poles to the Kick and Glide......51
    Chapter 5: Basic Turns: Step and Skate............57
    Chapter 6: Getting Up and Down Hills.............67

Part II: Basic Off-Track Techniques

    Introduction......................................89
    Chapter 7: Off-Track Kick and Glide..............91
    Chapter 8: Steps and Skates......................97
    Chapter 9: Off-Track Uphills.....................101
    Chapter 10: Off-Track Miscellaneous..............109

Part III: Cross-Country Downhill Skiing

    Introduction....................................117
    Chapter 11: Advanced Turning...................119

Part IV: Advanced Track Technique

    Introduction....................................139
    Chapter 12: Focusing on the Diagonal............141

Part V: Conditioning

    Introduction....................................165
    Chapter 13: Cardiovascular Training.............167
    Chapter 14: Conditioning Muscle Groups..........175

Suggested Readings..................................191

To: The Klister Corner gang: Dennis, Marilyn, Bob, Sim and Irish.

With special thanks to:
    John Alarie—Fisher of America
    Rainer Jansson—Exel-Silente
    Charlie Levin—Salomon North America
    Butch Widen—Odlo USA

If you can walk you can ski—a pleasantly inaccurate aphorism. Unfortunately, man doesn't take automatically to cross-country skiing. Certain basics must be mastered to become a proficient cross-country skier. The more technique learned and perfected, the more enjoyable each day of cross-country skiing becomes.

Technique and a solid foundation of the basic skills are important no matter what type of cross-country skiing you plan to do. Too often technique is shrugged off as something only racers have to learn, but even the most experienced expedition skiers and top cross-country downhill practitioners are steeped in the fundamentals of good cross-country ski technique.

This book is about basic and intermediate technique the way it is taught in America. We have learned a great deal about teaching cross-country skiing since the sport first became popular in the early 1970's. Norwegian, Swedish and Finnish instructors helped us get started in the cross-country teaching game, but soon our Yankee ingenuity had us experimenting with more effective ways of translating technical information into easily understood and learned techniques.

There are no chapters on equipment, snow camping, expedition skiing or racing. That material is best left to other books and the annual cross-country magazines. The goal of this book is to transform a ski walker, hiker, plodder or shuffler into a kicking and gliding skier. This, then, is a self help book, one to carry along onto the snow.

With this book you can learn on your own but, as technique improves, be sure to consult with a qualified PSIA (Professional Ski Instructors of America) teacher for a critique. While I can get you started towards better technique, nothing beats the personal touch and helpful hints received in person from a good instructor.

Good luck and better skiing days!

Bob Woodward

PART I

BASIC CROSS-COUNTRY TECHNIQUES

1

TO THE TRACKS

The best place to learn and practice cross-country ski technique is on a well prepared track. If you're lucky, there will be a touring center near home or machine set tracks in a local park or on the athletic fields of a nearby school. If, however, you have no touring center close to home or snow is a few hours drive away, you have to learn to make your own tracks in which to practice.

When you get on snow, find a section of flat terrain about twenty-five meters long. Ski-walk up and down this section several times packing in two parallel grooves for the skis and solid areas alongside the grooves for pole plants (refer to Fig. 1).

There are many reasons why the use of tracks is best for learning. You don't have to glue your eyes to the snow as you would off-track to see what will happen next, and the skis are guided along by the tracks, allowing you to concentrate on technique. The tracks provide you with the opportunity to develop the basic kick and glide technique without worrying about your skis sinking down into the snow on each kick and lurching forward on each glide. A well prepared track provides a solid base on which to learn. Learning on-track is like learning to drive a car on a paved road versus learning to drive on a mud covered backwoods logging road (off track).

Many experienced tour skiers are amazed how badly they ski their first time on prepared tracks. Quite simply, they have learned to plod through deeper snow rather than how to ski. Sometimes a disgruntled long time tour skier will say, "Well, track skiing is only for racers." Not so. The best racers, exercise skiers and tourers alike learn the fundamentals on tracks and then adapt them to that segment of the sport in which they are most interested.

The surest way to become a graceful cross-country skier is to put in practice time on tracks. A typical example of this is my friend, Cheryl. A fine cross-country downhill skier and backcountry tourer, Cheryl tried track skiing with embarrassing results. She flailed instead of making fluid movements. She felt intimidated.

Cheryl's answer was to take as many advanced ski lessons as possible. Fortunately her instructor took her aside after the second lesson and said, "More lessons won't make you a better skier. You know what to work on and only practice time on the snow will make you a better skier." She put in the time and became a better skier.

Not everyone has the time to devote to perfecting their cross-country skiing, but the more time spent on tracks perfecting basic techniques the better. Cross-country skiing is an easy sport to learn. A little technique goes a long way toward providing lots of fun. The move up from beginner/intermediate to advanced skier is a quantum leap. That leap is greatly shortened by on-track practice.

Dennis Oliphant is the first subject for the sequence and still photos. The reason for choosing him is simple; he typifies the best of cross-country skiing and ski instruction (refer to Fig. 2).

An all-around skier, Dennis tours, backpacks on skis, is a crack telemark and cross-country downhill skier, and has raced at the top citizens' level both here and abroad. He does it all well.

But his best quality is his sense of humor and upbeat personality. He doesn't, as many do, take ski instruction as an ultra serious matter akin to teaching the catechism. Teaching is fun and Dennis tries to keep his students on their toes with good teaching and fast one-liners. He is successful. His students come away with a good feeling about cross-country skiing and the realization that while having fun they have learned a great deal.

If an instructor scowls and tends to run his class like a seminar in early Greek drama, beat a hasty retreat. Instruction has to be enjoyable for teacher and student.

FIG. 1

FIG. 2: *Dennis Oliphant.*

2

THE DIAGONAL STRIDE

The diagonal stride is the heart of all cross-country ski technique. The term 'diagonal' confuses many people. So let's describe the move as "kick and glide." Kick on one ski and glide on the other. This is easily recognized when you see a good skier moving over the terrain in long, smooth strides.

The best way to learn the kick and glide technique is to start by working without skis on the all-important weight shift. Weight shift—remember that term because it is the most important element in the kick and glide and most other phases of cross-country technique. In the kick and glide, the key is shifting the entire weight from one ski to the other. Incomplete or partial weight shifts result in poor technique.

The stationary kick done without skis is an excellent way of getting the feel of a total weight shift. In Figures 3 and 4, notice how Dennis stands in place with his left foot and swings his right foot to and fro. His arms swing along naturally; the opposite arm and leg move together just as in walking.

Try this exercise to get the feel of having all the weight committed to one leg. Alternate legs frequently and check to make sure the arms swing naturally as in the photos. The only difference on snow with skis is that as the swinging (kicking) leg comes forward, it will be weighted to push the ski down the track for glide.

Moving onto skis, take a look at the photos following in this section. Notice that Dennis is not using his poles. Poles are a hindrance rather than a help at this point in learning, so drop them beside the track (refer to Fig. 5).

Without poles try the basic kick phase of the kick and glide. With one leg, make a series of short, down and back kicks to propel yourself down the practice track. Alternate legs to get a feeling of the kicking movement. Try to put all the weight onto the kicking leg with each kick, then shift it to the other leg (resting leg) before the next quick, down and back kick.

After this exercise, bring both legs into play to get familiar with the glide phase of the kick and glide. Push down and back with the right leg, after it has extended backward, bring it forward, shift your weight onto it and push the ski down the track for glide. Keep your weight shifted onto the gliding ski for a moment, then quickly shift to the left ski for a kick. Repeat a series of kicks and glides down the track, exaggerating the shift from kicking ski to gliding ski as you move along. Keep your knees bent and stay in a slightly crouched body position.

Up to this point, we have concentrated on the lower body. Now let's add the arms. Most people think they have to make elaborate maneuvers with their arms in cross-country skiing. In truth, the arms act just as they do in walking; they move from front to rear in natural unison with their opposite leg.

Be aware of two common arm faults: same arm same leg movement, and fascist arms. The first fault is frequent and unnatural. As the right leg kicks, the skier moves his right arm backward. Left arm and leg go in the same direction. The result, stiff unbalanced movement not unlike that of the fictional character Frankenstein (refer to Fig. 6).

Fascists arms are stiff forward and backward arm swings like the arm movements popular with some soldiers during World War II. Stiff arms make for uncomfortable, unstable skiing movements. Keep your arms relaxed and swinging naturally (refer to Fig. 7).

To integrate the arm and leg movements best, start kick and glide practice runs with short, shuffling movements. When all the limbs are coordinated, extend out into a longer stride.

I call the short, choppy arm and leg movement, "Latin dancing." It's like a samba. The quick, short tempo is a real help in getting relaxed and started down the track properly (refer to Fig. 8, 9, 10, 11 and 12).

Now, ski up and down the track a few times to get the idea of the weight shift in the legs and the smooth rhythmic motion of the arms. While practicing, try to incorporate these pointers:

- As comfort and ease increase, ski in a more erect body position with the shoulders rolled slightly inward, head up and eyes looking down the track about ten feet.

- Reduce the exaggerated bend in the knees (bend the knee over the lead ski just enough that the leg is supporting your weight comfortably).
- Keep the arms moving straight down the track, not crossing the chest or waving them out to the side (refer to Fig. 13).
- Get a song going in your head. This helps establish a rhythmic kick and glide (refer to Fig. 14).

You're bound to try too hard, or have your skis suddenly stop doing what you ask of them during this first practice session. This usually means a fall into the snow. Falling is almost as important as getting up.

I believe that the rear is the most important part of the human anatomy. It will take a beating much better than a leg, arm or head. Try to fall, if possible, backward and let the rear cushion your fall.

To get up, witness Dennis rising from a tumble. He rolls over onto his knees, places his hands out for support, comes up to one knee and stands erect. You should be able to execute this maneuver without poles. Getting up with poles will come later and should be easier (refer to Fig. 15, 16, 17 and 18).

FIG. 3: Practice the basic kick without skis to get the feel of a total weight shift.

FIG. 4

FIG. 5: *With one leg make a series of short, down and back kicks to propel yourself down the track.*

FIG. 6: *Do not move the arm and leg on the same side of the body in the same direction.*

FIG. 7: *Avoid exaggerated, stiff arm movements.*

FIG. 8: Start into a fully extended kick and glide with a short, shuffling motion.

FIG. 9

FIG. 10

FIG. 11

FIG. 12

THE DIAGONAL STRIDE

FIG. 13: *Keep your arms moving straight down the track (a), not across your body (b).*

FIG. 14

FIG. 15: *Getting up from a fall.*

FIG. 16

FIG. 17

FIG. 18

3

FIRST MOVEMENT WITH POLES

As mentioned earlier, poles can hamper basic technique if brought into play too soon. Before adding them to the kick and glide make sure your poles are the proper length and that you know how to get into the straps properly (refer to Fig. 19).

Use the following measuring technique as you stand on your skis; place the tip of one pole just behind the heel of one boot and insert the pole's grip up under your arm pit. If the top of the pole's grip rests snugly under your arm pit without pushing your shoulder up in the air, the pole is the proper size. If the pole pushes your arm up in the air, it is too long. If the top of the pole comes nowhere near your arm pit, the pole is too short.

To put the poles on properly, insert the hands up through the straps as shown in the photograph (refer to Fig. 20).

There are left and right hand poles, a fact that amazes most skiers. To know which pole is which, look at the pole straps. Two straps emanate from the pole grip. The lower strap loops around the outside of the hand; the upper strap goes around the thumb and across the back of the hand.

Right and left sorted out and put on properly? Make sure the straps are properly tightened so the pole will dangle between the thumb and forefinger as shown in Figure 21. The fit between the thumb and forefinger should not hurt; it should be a comfortably tight fit. If the pole strap is properly adjusted, the pole will dangle down without being held by your fingers. The pole will be an extension of your arm (refer to Fig. 22).

Getting this adjustment correct is very important for the techniques we will be discussing from this point on. In these techniques (double pole, kick double pole, diagonal stride with poles), the poles are released as they pass the legs following a push for power. With tightened straps, the poles should extend naturally to the rear as necessary appendages to the arms, without retrieval problems.

If the poles have straps that come right out of the top of the grip instead of ¾ of an inch lower, it will be impossible to keep the pole snugged in the crook of the hand. This problem can be remedied by taping the straps down as shown in the illustration (refer to Fig. 23).

Now let's get to the first movement of poles—the *double pole*. Double poling is the best way to propel yourself along slight downhills or to gain speed on the flats. In off-track touring, the double pole often gives the skier a much needed rest from pack chaffing, kick and glide skiing.

The basic body movement in the double pole is reminiscent of those toy birds that, when set on the edge of a water glass, endlessly bend over, dip their beaks into the water and pop back up. That's the essence of the double pole technique; bend at the waist and pop back up. Unlike the birds, you have the added responsibility of pushing down on your poles as you bring your upper body down towards your skis.

Look at the photo sequence of Figures 24, 25 and 26. Dennis starts by bringing his poles up (arms bent naturally); he plants them (notice the backward angle so they come in right by his boots), and as he pushes on his poles for power, he begins to bend his upper torso. He releases the poles as they pass his legs and, because his pole straps are tight, the poles stay securely attached to his hands.

On your flat practice track, propel yourself along using the double pole technique. Keep these tips in mind:

- Keep your head up so you can see where you're going. Don't drop it down (refer to Fig. 27, 28).
- Try not to sit as you make your double pole movement. Sitting is inefficient. Bend at the waist (refer to Fig. 29, 30).
- Remember to release your poles as they pass your legs (refer to Fig. 31).
- Push on your poles until you release them. Don't make exaggerated rearward pushes as Dennis does in Figure 32.
- Try not to flare your poles out in front. Study the sequence shots and attempt to bring the poles up just as Dennis does in the second frame.

Remember: strive for economy of movement. No flashy, flailing arm motions.

The other double pole movement is called the *kick double pole*. Harder to learn, the kick double pole takes time to master, but can be very useful on flat terrain and slight downhills where you are not going fast enough to use the straight double pole technique. The kick double pole is also very restful.

The name gives away the difference between this technique and the double pole. The kick with one leg adds the extra speed discussed above. Dennis demonstrates a step by step exercise designed to teach you the fundamental movements of the kick double pole (refer to Fig. 33, 34, and 35).

He starts from a standing position with his hands out, ready to bring the poles out to plant them in the snow. As he brings his poles up and plants them, he kicks his right leg back. As he pushes down on his poles for power, he brings the right ski back in alongside the left ski and finishes up his double poling motion.

It is an open and closed scissor motion—open, raise up onto the poles and kick one leg back; close, compress the upper body down, push down on the poles and bring the trailing leg back in for the glide phase. Synchronization of these movements is all important. Too often skiers tend to kick the leg early or late, throwing it out of sequence with the upper body movements.

I suggest you work on the technique periodically integrating it slowly into your bag of tricks. This technique takes time. Give yourself time to master it. Do the stationary exercise before each attempt at the technique on your practice track.

As mentioned earlier, always try to fall on your rear. Since we've added some new movements to your basic technique repertoire, a few out-of-control falls are to be expected. So think about going back on your rear instead of forward onto your nose when you get that wobbly, "Oh no, I'm about to fall" feeling.

Dennis demonstrates the proper way to rise up from the snow with your poles on (refer to Fig. 36, 37 and 38). You may be one of those people who find the poles a nuisance in getting up from the snow. They always seem to tangle you up rather than help. For those who feel this way even after trying Dennis' approach to the standing up problem, try this technique:

- Remove your poles.
- Lay them together on one side.
- Push on them with both hands to get onto your knees.
- On your knees, take a pole in either hand. Grasp the poles mid way down their shafts and push on them to help you up to a fully erect position.

FIG. 19: *Checking to see if the poles are the proper length.*

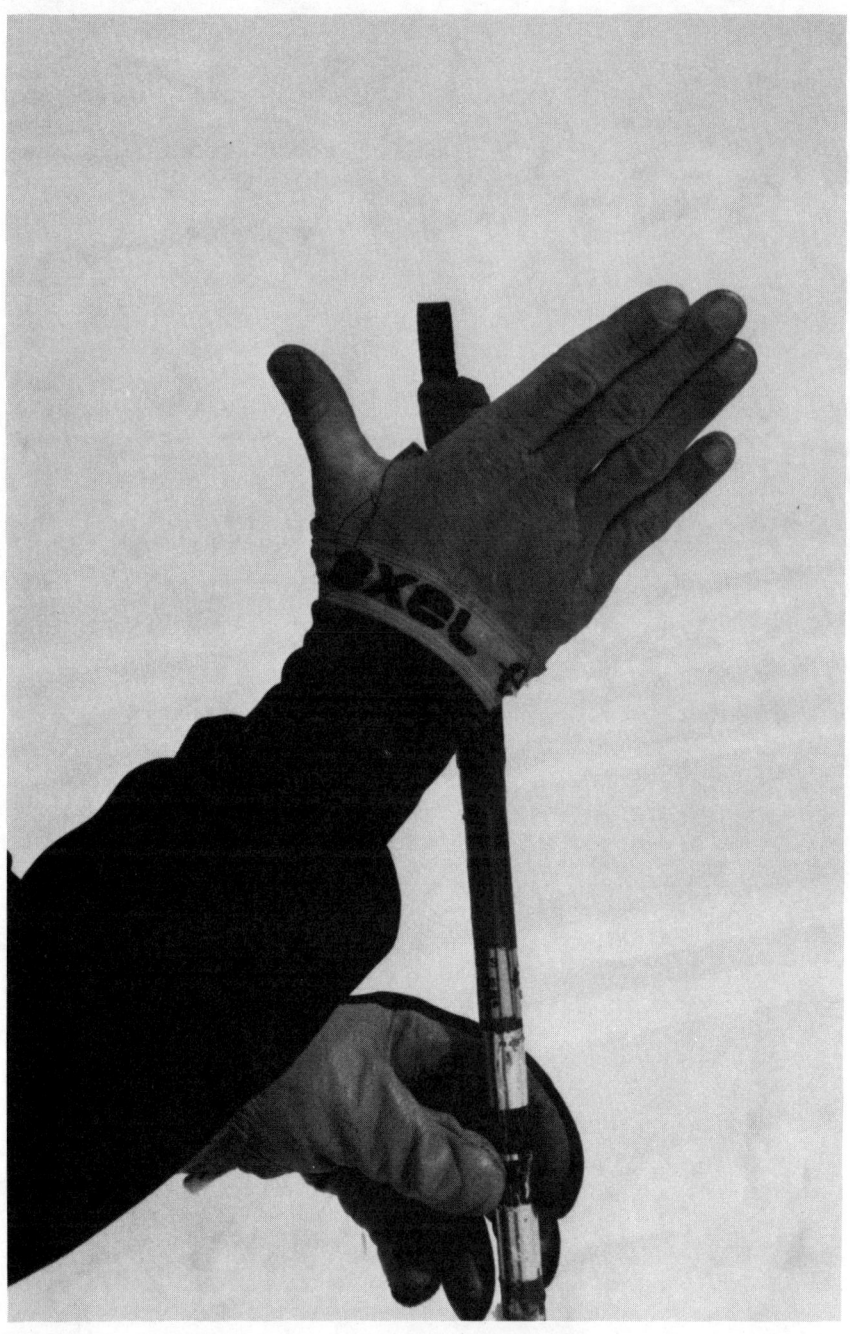

FIG. 20: *The proper way to grip your poles.*

FIG. 21: *Yes, there are right and left hand poles—the straps tell the story.*

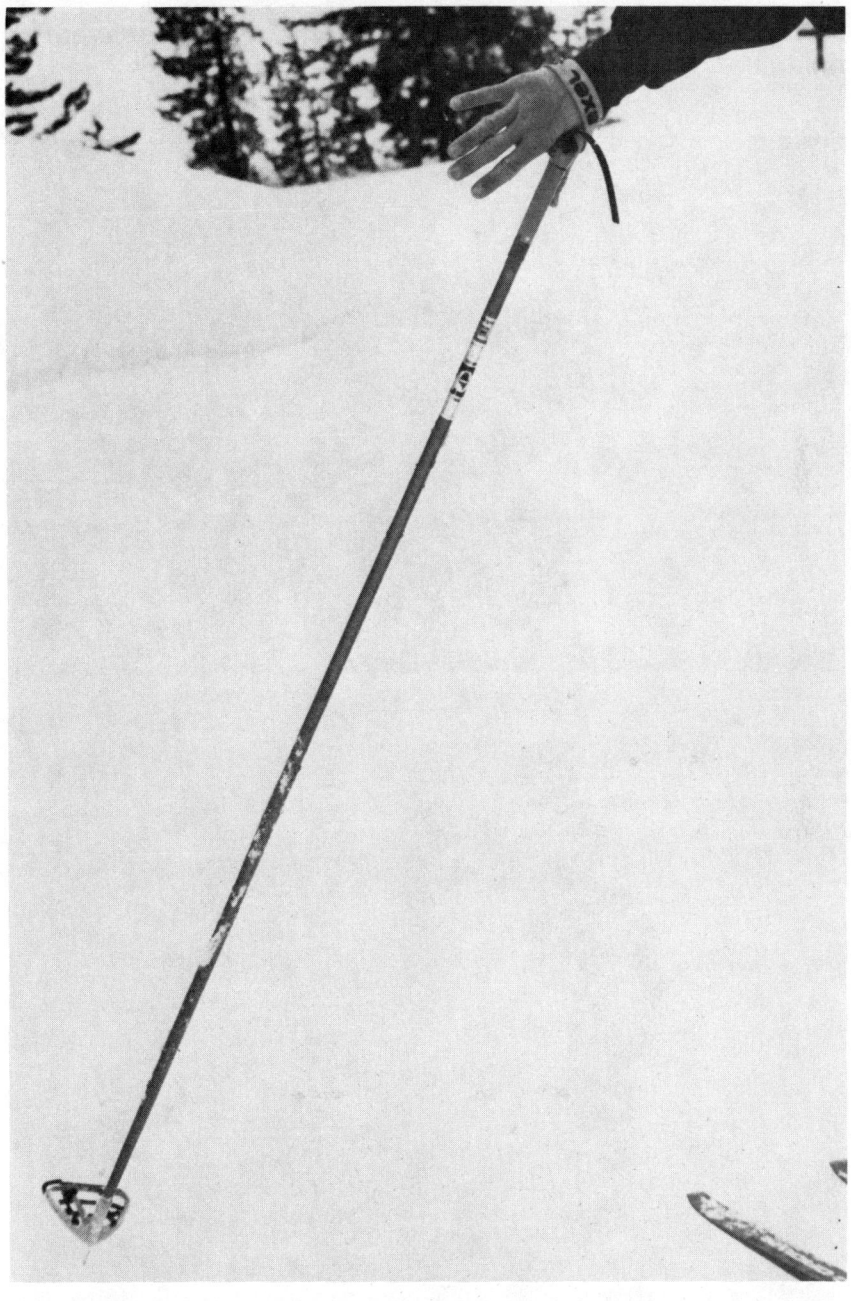

FIG. 22: Dangle the pole from your grip to make sure it fits snuggly into the crook of your hand.

FIG. 23: *Tape the pole straps down (right) if they come out of the top of the pole's grip.*

FIG. 24: *The basic double pole: come up onto poles, push down, and compress the upper body.*

FIG. 25

FIG. 26

FIG. 27: *Head up, not down, for better double poling.*

FIG. 28

FIRST MOVEMENT WITH POLES

FIG. 29

FIG. 30: *Compress the upper body—don't sit back and down.*

FIG. 31: *Release the poles from your grip as they pass your legs.*

FIG. 32: *Exaggerated poling motions waste energy.*

FIG. 33: *The three step stationary kick double pole practice routine.*

FIG. 34

FIG. 35

FIG. 36: *Getting up from a fall with poles on.*

FIG. 37

FIRST MOVEMENT WITH POLES

FIG. 38

4

ADDING THE POLES TO THE KICK AND GLIDE

Now we'll "up the ante" by adding poles into the kick and glide technique. Most people think that when you add the poles to the diagonal, you automatically have to make wildly exaggerated arm movements—not so. Keep the arms moving naturally in their front-to-rear pendulum motion.

Consider the following arm concepts before starting to practice your diagonal with poles:

- A bent arm is more powerful on a pole plant than a stiff arm. Test this theory by holding an arm out stiff and then pushing down as hard as possible with the pole against the snow. Now try the same push on the pole with a naturally bent arm. You'll have much more power and control with the naturally bent arm.
- When you plant the pole for power, it should be angled to the rear so the basket comes in right beside your feet. Release the pole from your grip as it passes your leg and let it extend naturally to the rear along with your arm movement.

Now let's look at Dennis as he adds poles to his diagonal. As he brings his right arm forward it is bent naturally. He pushes on the right pole for power. Notice the acute rearward angle so the pole comes in near his feet and how he releases the pole as it passes his legs (refer to Fig. 39, 40, 41).

ADDING THE POLES TO THE KICK AND GLIDE

In this sequence, Dennis is stretched out in a comfortable stride. For best results when you start practicing the kick and glide with poles, start with a "Latin dance" shuffle, and build into an elongated stride (refer to Fig. 42, 43, 44 and 45).

The "Latin dance" shuffle helps coordinate arm and leg movements. Get a solid rhythm established, making sure the opposite arm and leg are working in unison. Once secure with this shuffling movement, try to stretch out into a longer stride.

Practice the shuffle-into-stride sequence up and down your practice track. Consider these tips as you move along.

- Notice in the sequence shots of the shuffle-into-stride how Dennis' body is erect and his knees are bent excessively while shuffling. As he breaks into the strike, he tilts his body forward down the track and rises up so his knees are not bent as much. Try to do the same in your practice.
- Move from the short arm swings into the longer, smoother arm swings as shown in the sequence photos. Do not "throw" your poles away at the end of each arm swing or bring them forward stiffly with locked elbows. Both of these mistakes are shown in Figure 46. Both make for inefficient and tiresome technique.

I am particularly opposed to the "throwing" the poles away technique that has been taught for years by other instructors. The popular myth was that if you taught skiers to "throw" their poles away at the end of each stroke, they would learn the importance of letting their arm extend naturally to the rear. Unfortunately all "throwing" does is create wildly flailing arm movements that are hard to correct. "Throwing" also directs too much physical energy backward instead of forward down the track.

FIG. 39: *The diagonal (kick and glide) with poles.*

FIG. 40

ADDING THE POLES TO THE KICK AND GLIDE

FIG. 41

FIG. 42: *"Latin dancing" into a full stride.*

FIG. 43

FIG. 44

FIG. 45

FIG. 46: *Throwing the poles away and reaching forward with stiff locked arms.*

5

BASIC TURNS: STEP AND SKATE

The two most often used cross-country ski turns are the step and the skate. Their relationship to each other is much like that of the double pole and kick double pole. One maneuver (double pole step turn) is basic and easy to learn; the other technique (kick double pole skate) is more difficult to master and is more technical.

The Step Turn

Dennis demonstrates the basic step turn in Figures 47 and 48. In the first frame, he puts all his weight on his left ski and steps off to the right. As the right ski comes down, his weight shifts to it, and he quickly brings the left ski over. Once the two skis are together, he distributes his weight over them equally.

Before trying the step turn, go through the stationary exercise shown in Figures 49, 50 and 51. To practice, put your weight on your right ski and lift the left ski up off the snow. Now, step to the left, and weight the left ski. Bring the right ski over and equalize the weight on the skis.

Do this exercise slowly at first and as you become more comfortable with it, do it more rapidly. Keep your hands out in front as Dennis does in the photos and keep your knees bent.

Now try a few step turns on your prepared practice course. Move along making one step to the right, then one to the left. When comfortable with single step turns, try making a series of turns in one direction, then in the other direction.

Remember to keep the hands out and knees bent. If you tuck your arms in close to your body and stand with straight knees, you'll be top heavy and primed for a fall.

Don't use the poles initially. Add them as confidence is gained. When you are ready to try poling during the turn, plant the pole on the inside of the turn (right pole/right turn—left pole/left turn) for added support during the turn.

If you become unstable during a step turn, try not to rely on your poles but on your knees. A good deep bend in the knees can turn an unstable turn into a stable one. keep the knees flexed and ready.

The Skate Turn

The skate turn uses techniques similar to those employed by hockey players and speed skaters to propel themselves across the ice. It differs from the step turn in three distinct areas:

- Body position; lower "action" crouch is used (refer to Fig. 52).
- Thrust; the pushing-off ski is edged inward for more bite and the skier puts more "umph" into the leg before bringing it across. Instead of stepping over, you are pushing yourself off in a new direction (refer to Fig. 53).
- Poling; each skating movement is accompanied by a double pole.

Figure 54 shows Dennis in the skate crouch position with his hands (forward and slightly out to the side) coming forward for the double pole. As the trailing ski is edged for grip, he starts his leg thrust and at the same time pushes through on his poles to complete the double poling movement.

Skate turns are not particularly important for general touring. They are very important, however, for advanced track skiing and racing. It is good to practice them because the skating technique opens the doors to general skating as a method of over-the-snow travel.

Often you'll have one of those days when the snow is perfect and you can skate along for miles. To me, this is one of the greatest experiences in cross-country skiing. I recall days when a hard base was covered by a few inches of powder snow, or there were hard, unbreakable crusts or just a trace of corn snow over ice—conditions where we could skate for miles in any direction. It was exhiliarating!

In Figure 54, Dennis demonstrates the basic skate technique on the flat packed snow between the tracks, a good place to practice the technique. Skate along, moving rhythmatically from side to side, with a song in your head to give you the timing.

Start by keeping your poles off the snow. As you become proficient with the skate technique, double pole on every skate for even more side-to-side thrust.

The secret to successful skating, as with the step turn, is to keep your knees bent and flexible.

FIG. 47: *The basic step turn.*

FIG. 48

FIG. 49: *Step turn stationary practice.*

FIG. 50

FIG. 51

FIG. 52: *Getting ready to skate.*

FIG. 53: *The more dynamic action of the skate.*

FIG. 54: *Skating along.*

6

GETTING UP AND DOWN HILLS

Nothing intimidates more when starting cross-country skiing than the ups and downs along the trail. Ups actually mean agonizing slips with face prints on the snow. With downs, the fear of falling is ever present.

A phased approach makes learning ups and downs easier and safer. The approach works this way; start with a basic uphill technique and follow it with a basic downhill technique. This approach leads into slightly more advanced uphill and downhill techniques; soon you'll have mastered all the techniques required until you take up advanced cross-country downhill skiing.

The first phase is the *shuffle up—straight run down.* As you recall, the "Latin dance" shuffle is important in learning the kick and glide technique. The shuffle is not only a good way of synchronizing your arms and legs for the kick and glide, but also for getting up gently sloping hills (refer to Fig. 55, 56).

Let's say you are kicking and gliding along the track in a long, smooth gait. Ahead you see a short hill of moderate incline. At the base of the hill you break into the short shuffle step as shown in the pictures. Your tempo increases and you make choppier movements with both your arms and legs. Notice that Dennis flexes his knees more and drops his hands down. This helps get his body weight down onto his skis, thus ensuring that the wax or waxless pattern of the skis' underfoot will get positive purchase on the snow with each kick.

Once reaching the top of the practice rise, turn around and prepare for a straight running downhill. In Figure 57, Dennis gets in a low crouch and places his hands out to the side for added stability. I call this arm and hand positioning the "ready" position. Keep the terminology in mind because it will come up again and again as we progress.

Notice also that Dennis has his weight equally distributed on each ski. The weight on each ski is centered in the area from the balls of his feet back to his heels.

Try a few straight running downhills after your uphill shuffles. Incorporate these ideas as you become more confident:

- Bounce a few times at the start of the run to make sure your knees are flexing.
- Bounce up and down as you descend the incline. This teaches you to relax and to absorb the changes in terrain with your knees.
- Tuck your poles under your arms to be more aerodynamic. If you feel unstable, bring them back into the "ready" position (refer to Fig. 58).

Also learn the proper high speed fall as demonstrated by Dennis in Figures 59, 60 and 61.

Herringbone/Snowplow

The herringbone is still the finest way to proceed uphill when the incline becomes too steep, or your wax or waxless pattern isn't working. While it may feel awkward to begin with, the herringbone is easily assimilated into anyone's technique.

The uphill herringbone begins with a splaying of the skis out into a "v" shape. Next, roll the ankles in so that the skis edge into the snow for grip. Bend the knees inward as if grasping a basketball between them. Now you're ready to start walking uphill. Plant one ski, weight it, and make sure your grip is secure before you begin lifting the opposite ski up the hill (refer to Fig. 62, 63, 64, 65).

What about the poles? Look at the photos of Dennis making a herringbone. As he starts to step up with his right ski, he puts pressure on his left pole. Notice how the poles are set about a foot out from each boot and Dennis' arms are in the ready position. Once the right ski and arm have moved up the hill, Dennis will anchor the ski by edging it into the snow, and he'll push on the right pole as he begins to bring the left ski up.

At the top of your practice hill, get set to try a new technique—the snowplow—to get down. Almost everyone with alpine (downhill) skiing experience knows how to snowplow. It is the most basic alpine and cross-country downhill position.

To initiate your snowplow down the hill, invert the "v" used in the uphill herringbone. Place your ski tips close together and spread the tails of your skis wide apart. Bend your knees and ankles inward to edge the skis into the snow (refer to Fig. 66).

With your hands in the "ready" position, start sliding down the hill. If your speed increases, push out on your heels. This will edge your skis inward, digging them into the snow to slow you down. Pushing out on your heels exerts a great deal of strain on the muscles on the inside of your thighs. Since these muscles are infrequently used, they will be sore after a good session of snowplowing.

Work on your snowplow and after you feel comfortable with it, try this exercise:

- Start off in a straight running position. Descend the slope until your speed increases, then move into the snowplow position to slow down.
- Move in and out of these two downhill positions as you descend.

This exercise gives you the idea of switching in and out of position while moving, and introduces you to the practicality of the snowplow as a braking technique.

Sidestep/Snowplow Turn

When the hills become too steep, sidestepping is the only way up. At the base of the steep incline stand sideways to the hill. Then follow these basic steps (refer to Fig. 67):

- Step and reach up the hill with the uphill ski and pole.
- Plant the uphill ski and pole securely, and put all your weight on them as you bring up the trailing ski and pole.
- After bringing up the downhill (trailing) ski and pole, weight them and make your next step up the hill.

Make these movements quick and positive. Work from the strongest side. If the right leg is stronger, use the left ski to lead up the hill and vice versa.

If the slope becomes too steep or slick, angle the knees into the slope. By pushing the knees into the hill, you increase the angle of the skis' edges for better grip.

Often you'll start up a hill only to find it is steeper than you bargained for. The sidestep is the best steep hill ascent method, but if you have started up in the herringbone and want to change over, follow the sequence shots and try this method (refer to Fig. 68):

- Plant your poles behind your rear as shown.
- Put all your weight on the poles and start making a quick series of steps to one or the other side.

- With both skis over, and perpendicular to the slope, weight them carefully, and when secure, bring the poles over and set them into the snow for additional anchoring.
- Proceed up the hill via the side step.

Now to get back down, let's try making left and right turns from the snowplow position. Start down the hill in your snowplow position. As you move along, start pushing aggressively on your left heel while rotating your upper torso slightly to the right. Let your hands lead you through the turn just as Dennis does in Figures 69, 70 and 71. Push and steer and you have made a right turn!

After another climb up the hill, try a left turn. Press on the right ski with your heel to edge it and start it turning. Steer with your hands to the left while rotating your upper torso in that direction to complete the left turn.

Practice snowplow turns to the left and right and then complete the workout with the *half-plow technique* in the tracks. The half-plow technique is good for slowing down on tracked corners and downhills. Dennis demonstrates how to perform the half-plow technique in Figure 72:
- Shift one ski out of the track and put most of your weight on it.
- Keep your weight on it and push vigorously on the heel until you slow down.
- Once your speed is down, bring the ski back over into the groove on the tracks and ski on!

FIG. 55: *Getting up a short hill with the shuffle step.*

FIG. 56

FIG. 57: *The basic straight running downhill position.*

FIG. 58: *A more aerodynamic half tuck.*

FIG. 59: *A high speed fall using the rear effectively.*

FIG. 60

FIG. 61

FIG. 62: *Three rear views of the herringbone—skis planted (a); right leg moving uphill (b); right leg planted, left leg beginning to lift for move up (c).*

FIG. 63

FIG. 64

FIG. 65: *Front view of basic herringbone position.*

FIG. 66: *The snowplow position.*

FIG. 67: *Sidestepping position.*

FIG. 68: *The start of a changeover from a herringbone to sidestep.*

FIG. 69: *Executing a snowplow turn.*

FIG. 70

FIG. 71

FIG. 72: *For safe in-track downhills, plow one ski out of the track to brake your speed.*

PART II

BASIC OFF-TRACK TECHNIQUES

Introduction

For many cross-country skiers, touring along in ankle deep snow through silent woods remains the essence of the sport. Far from the crowds, you glide quietly over the snow, witnessing nature in one of her more magic moods.

While beautiful, off-track skiing can also be hard work. You need to adapt the ski techniques learned on-track to account for deep snows and the fact that you might be carrying a day, or expedition, pack.

In this section, the techniques learned on-track will be adapted to off-track. Off-track ski movements are quicker, more subtle, and often more muscular. Off-track ski techniques also change as the snow depth changes. Skiing on hard pack is as easy as skiing on tracks; skiing in deep powder or mush is much more difficult. Let's look at each phase of basic technique and see how to change it for better off-track touring.

7

*O*FF-*T*RACK *K*ICK AND *G*LIDE

When the snowpack is solid and covered with an inch or two of powder, mush or corn snow, the basic on-track ski techniques will work perfectly. You may have to adapt them slightly, like skiing a wider stance to account for the lack of parallel tracked grooves guiding your skis, but in general, the techniques learned in Part I will suffice.

Once the snow gets up around your ankles, however, different techniques have to be used to move along efficiently. One of the most effective techniques for deeper snow travel is the *shuffle*.

The shuffling kick and glide works off-track because it is often impossible to weight and unweight your skis fully, or to push down on your poles forcefully in deeper snow with a softer base underfoot. If you overweight either a ski or a pole in soft untracked snow, you'll end up falling.

So we'll concentrate on an advanced form of shuffling; a form midway between the "Latin dance" and the fully extended kick and glide. This shuffle is made with quick shifts in weight from ski to ski. Just as you are about to commit your total weight to the kicking or gliding ski, you shift it. The poles are carried further to the side for stability as you move along.

Dennis demonstrates the off-track shuffle in Figures 73, 74 and 75. His arms are held further out to the side and his arm and leg motions are choppier than in the fully extended kick and glide. He's bouncing from one ski onto the next, avoiding too much weight on either ski. The slight bouncing action is necessary to bring the kicking ski into quick contact with the snow for grip and to allow the gliding ski to punch its way forward through the snow pack.

If the snow is deeper, the *lurch and lunge* technique is helpful. Take a look at Figures 76 and 77. In the first frame, Dennis lurches upward bringing his left ski out of the snow. After the ski is free from the snow, he lunges forward onto it driving it into a glide. His entire weight goes onto the gripping ski to get purchase with his wax or waxless pattern. After a quick push backward for propulsion, he springs upward and lunges forward to put the left ski into a glide.

At the end of a short glide, Dennis will try to make a firm kick down on the ski to start the lurch and lunge process all over again.

Lurching and lunging along is hard work and this technique should therefore only be used when absolutely necessary. If you have to get somewhere in a hurry and the snow is knee high, use the lurch and lunge. Otherwise, use the less taxing *groucho*.

Dennis shows us the basic groucho position in Figure 78. He flexes his knees and drops his body down. Using the front leg to push against the snow (imagine it knee high), he slinks along. When you try this technique, think of Groucho Marx' famous movie walk, and you'll have the technique mastered in no time flat.

FIG. 73: *Off-track shuffling—often the only way to move through ankle deep snow.*

FIG. 74

FIG. 75

FIG. 76: *Lurch and lunge.*

FIG. 77

FIG. 78: *The "Groucho."*

8

STEPS AND SKATES

In deep off-track snow conditions, the step turn is the most effective turn. Because of the unstable nature of untracked snow, each step must be sharp, without hesitation, without weight on one ski for too long. If overweighted, the ski will sink quickly down into the snow, throwing you off balance.

In Figures 79 and 80, Dennis descends the hill with his skis in a wide tracked (shoulder width apart) position for balance and support. His knees are bent to absorb changes in the terrain and snow depth and his hands are out in the "ready" position. Notice that as he makes a quick step to the right he is in a sitting position. This position allows his ski tips to ride up higher in the snow instead of diving. His hands remain in the "ready" position as he makes the step and the right pole, pressed against the snow, provides additional balance.

When practicing the step turn, keep the following tips in mind:

- Assume a sitting, downhill position.
- Wide track the skis (shoulder width).
- Hands at the "ready" position.
- Knees bent.
- Step fast and lively.

Step turns are easy and effective off-track; skates are impossible in deep snow. Save your skating turns for hard packed conditions or days when a few inches of snow cover a solid base.

FIG. 79: *Deep snow step turn.*

FIG. 80

9

OFF-TRACK UPHILLS

When it comes to gentle off-track uphills, drop the "Latin dance" quick shuffle for the more dynamic *"bigfoot"* technique. In the "bigfoot," attack the slope directly and rely on the wax or waxless pattern to give the purchase needed. Walking up the hill, lift each ski out of the snow with an exaggerated upward motion and slap it down hard for firm grip. Plant the poles firmly with each giant step for balance and power (refer to Fig. 81).

The temptation during first tries at this technique is to lean forward into the hill as the angle of the slope becomes steeper or the skis begin to slip. Leaning forward will send you onto your face. Do what doesn't come naturally; sit back on your heels and keep your upper body erect as Dennis does in the photo.

If the slope gets too steep, place your poles behind your rear as in the herringbone-to-sidestep technique. Place your palms over the tops of the poles and get a firm anchor in the snow with each giant step up the hill.

If you slip, compress your knees to bring your weight down more onto the skis with each step. The added weight on the skis should help compress the camber to make the wax or waxless pattern grip.

The herringbone and side-step are also very effective in off-track situations. Be sure to kick the skis free of the snow before attempting an upward step with either technique. If the snow is too deep to clear with a simple life of the skis, pulls up several times to clear a space for the ski in the snow. After clearing a space, step up with your herringbone or side-step.

If all the above climbing techniques fail or you face a long steep slope, try traversing to reach the top. Traversing a slope is the best line of attack to conquer a hill of any size easily (refer to Fig. 83, 84 and 85).

Starting out at an oblique angle to the slope, traverse across, while slowly ascending. After you've traversed some distance, stop, make a kick turn, and head off in the opposite direction. Continue this zigzagging course up the slope.

On steep sidehills, remove your hand from the strap of the uphill pole and grasp the pole midway down its shaft for better leverage and added stability (refer to Fig. 85).

If the hill you are traversing is hard packed or icy, make sure each ski and pole plant are made with authority. Should you fall in a situation like this, try to keep your skis perpendicular to the hill and your poles above your head as Dennis demonstrates in Fig. 86. In this position, the skis and poles will help break the fall.

FIG. 81: *Bigfooting uphill.*

FIG. 82: *Traversing uphill. Head up the hill at an oblique angle—stop—kick turn—and head off in a new direction.*

FIG. 83

FIG. 84

FIG. 85: *On steep sidehills remove hand from uphill pole grip and grasp the pole midway down its shaft.*

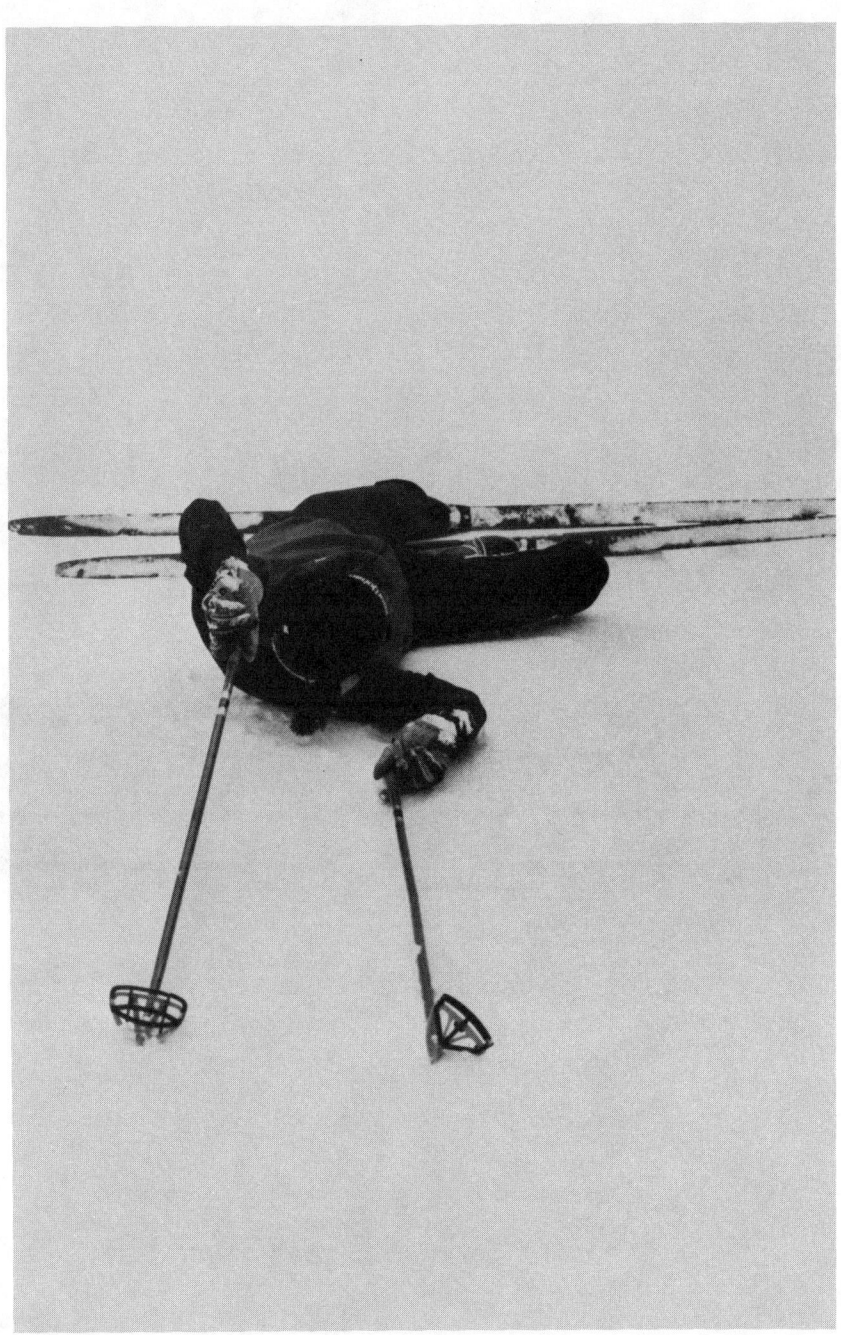

FIG. 86: *The best way to keep control on a steep hill fall.*

10

OFF-TRACK MISCELLANEOUS

Let's consider some special off-track situations: whiplash skiing, log and stream crossing, and falling and getting up with a pack.

At some point, you will be skiing along on an easy downgrade when suddenly your skis jet out from under you, tossing you backward. Or, just as you are about to fall, your skis screech to a near halt, throwing you suddenly forward. This is whiplash, or chiropractic ski conditions.

The problem is the skis are encountering different snow conditions or depths. The most common whiplash ski conditions come in the spring when the snow in sunny, exposed areas is slow mush, while the snow under the trees is fast ice. As you ski through the forest, you jerk back and forth uncomfortably. The same "herky-jerky" skiing happens in powder snow conditions when you ski from a thin cover of snow into deeper cover, or from pure powder into wind slap or crusted snow cover.

To remedy the whiplash skiing problem, try the following ideas: in spring snows, sit back on your heels, put one ski slightly ahead of the other and lower your body and hands down closer to the snow; in powder conditions, drop into the basic telemark position (as shown in Part III). The lower body position for spring conditions prepares you for sudden changes in speed. The telemark position makes the transition from one depth of snow to another easier.

Crossing Logs/Streams

Frozen streams, logs across the trail, and fences and stone walls require special maneuvers on skis.

It is easy to ford a narrow stream by putting one ski across the gap and planting it firmly on the other bank. With one ski across, plant both poles on the other side. Then place all the weight on the poles and the lead ski, swiftly bringing the other ski across. Dennis demonstrates this technique in Figures 87 and 88.

Rivers are more difficult to cross on cross-country skis. It's wise to step down the bank, making a firm track over which you can retreat. At the frozen water's edge, probe the poles to see if the snow or ice will stand up to some weight. Remember, fast moving water is slow to freeze to any depth. If the ice is two inches thick or thicker, it can usually take a skier's weight without problem.

If you judge the ice cover to be safe enough, sidestep out slowly, edging your way along. Make probes out to your side as you edge along. If the ice holds, ski along normally. On smooth ice, ski in as wide-tracked a position as possible, pushing yourself along with short, quick, double poling movements.

Small logs require a simple step up and over technique. Step up on to the log with one ski, move your poles up onto the log and dig them in. With your weight on the poles and the lead ski, bring the other ski up alongside. To get off, reverse the process; step down with one ski, bring the poles down and plant them on the snow, and then bring the other ski off the log.

Large logs or stone walls require a special technique and a willingness to get slightly cold or wet. Sit on the log or wall and roll over onto your back. Raise your skis up high over head, turn your body 180 degrees, and drop your skis on the other side, sitting back upright as you do so. If there are too many branches, you'll have to remove your skis and scramble over the log with skis in hand.

Some people try exotic machinations to go over post and rail fences. The easiest way is to take your skis off, slide between the rungs and while sitting on a rung, put the skis back on.

How about barbed wire fences? This is a problem some midwestern and many western tourers encounter. Here you can ask someone to hold the strands while you pass through as you normally would on foot during a dry season.

If the snow is deep and covers the bottom two strands of wire, step on the top strand, compressing it down with your ski: plant your poles on the other side of the fence and make a quick step over with the trailing ski.

Pack Problems

Falling is more of a problem when you have a pack on your back. The weight in the pack drives you deeper into the untracked snow and makes getting up more difficult.

Dennis has fallen in the powder. He removes his poles and makes an 'x' with them in the snow to give him support as he begins to rise. He takes his pack off and sets it well off to his side and out of the way. With the pack off and his poles placed for support, he can get up more easily (refer to Fig. 89, 90).

Once standing again, retrieve your pack, put it on and get your poles in place. Be sure to fasten the pack's waistbelt before moving on.

There are other pack problems, and the type of pack worn will often dictate your off-track technique. A fully loaded expedition softpack, or even a slightly loaded daypack, may prompt you to alter your basic techniques. The added weight of any pack and its tendency to sway while you ski can cause more sudden out-of-control movements. You have to ski many times with the pack of your choice to see how it rides and how it affects your technique.

If you plan to carry a pack on your daytrips, follow these suggestions:

- Use a day pack with some sort of waistbelt attachment to cut down on swaying.
- Use a daypack with padded shoulder straps to cut down on chaffing.
- Try a large fannypack instead of a day pack. Fannypacks interfere less with skiing movements and cause little or no chaffing.

For overnight or extended ski trips, always use a good internal frame softpack with a broad hipbelt. These packs can be adjusted to conform snugly to your body, eliminating as much pack sway as possible. Do not use a traditional frame pack. While great for summer hiking and backpacking, most framepacks sway side-to-side when used for cross-country ski backpacking.

FIG. 87: *Creek crossing technique.*

FIG. 88

FIG. 89: Getting up from a deep snow fall while wearing a pack. Remove the pack, plant your skis in an "x" configuration in the snow, and start up.

FIG. 90

PART III

CROSS COUNTRY DOWNHILL SKIING

Introduction

I've been dreading this section of the book because my view of cross-country downhill skiing seems to be antiquated—at least that's what the trend setters and "dyed-in-the-wool" telemarkers tell me. We differ in the amount of importance placed on telemarking and cross-country downhill skiing.

I think telemarking is fun. I also think using quasi-alpine skis, heavy rigid boots, special bindings and special poles just to make turns is dumb. I prefer making turns on the same equipment you use to tour. It's the skier, not the ski equipment, that makes turning fun.

This flies in the face of current theory which says if you buy specialized cross-country downhill equipment, you will become a better skier, making better turns. Where does this leave you if you want to get out for exercise on the tracks or take a long tour on skis? With several sets of equipment and an expensive investment.

Before you rush out and purchase specialized telemarking/cross-country downhill equipment, test some through a demo program at a ski shop or ski area. Try the gear on the prepared slopes and for touring and then make your purchasing decision.

In this section of the book, we'll look at basic cross-country downhill techniques done on general ski touring equipment. Also be prepared for simple language. I will not try to snow you with terms like "counter-rotation," "angulation" and "down the fall-line." "Just the facts," as Sergeant Friday used to say.

11

*A*DVANCED *T*URNING

Sideslipping

Knowledge of how to sideslip a steep slope should be a prerequisite before any cross-country skier moves onto other more advanced downhill techniques. Sideslipping is often the only effective method of descending a slope that is too steep, too icy, or too crusty for direct skiing.

Look at Figure 91 of Dennis in the basic sideslip position. His skis are perpendicular to the slope. Both skis are edged into the slope (inside edge of the downhill ski - outside edge of the uphill ski). His weight is equalized on the skis which allows them to slip sideways down the slope.

He pushes on his heels to start the skis sliding. A few bounces with the knees will also help this process. If the skis come to a halt, a quick hop gets them going again. If he goes too fast, he can weight the downhill ski and edge it to stop his movement.

The poles are held free of the snow while sliding. Use them only when necessary for balance or to help a stop.

Sitting/Traversing

Earlier we discussed the basic straight running downhill position and the sitting position for off-track powder downhills. The basic straight running position works best when you ski down short, mildly angled inclines with light snow cover. On slopes covered with deeper snow, use the sitting back position as shown in Figure 92.

Sit back with your weight on your heels and knees bent as if sitting in a chair. This allows your ski tips to ride higher in the snow, giving you more flotation. In this position, a deep snow downhill can be a slow, easy ride.

If that downhill ride becomes too fast, drag your poles through the snow to decelerate, or sit all the way down on your rear to stop. A good sit is the safest downhill stop.

Any slope that you find too intimidating should be traversed. We talked about the uphill traverse as a safe means of climbing a hill; the downhill traverse is simply the technique in reverse. Take a safe oblique angle across the slope; weight your downhill ski while allowing the uphill ski to ride a bit ahead and almost weight free. Sit back with your hands in the "ready" position and take off slowly. The angle of your descent will determine your downhill speed (refer to Fig. 93).

To stop or slow down, angle the uphill ski into the slope and weight it. As you swerve into the higher contour, your speed will begin to reduce. Some skiers make quick uphill step turns to accomplish the same thing. After stooping, kick turn and ski off at another oblique angle. Continue this zig-zagging route to the base of the hill.

Stem Christie

The natural progression from the basic turns learned in Part I begins with the stem christie. This is an old alpine ski turn that is most effective for cross-country skiing. Many consider it the most utilitarian turn on thin skis.

The stem christie starts from the snow plow. As you snowplow down a gentle slope, initiate the stem turn by first shifting your weight to the ski opposite the direction you wish to turn (right ski weighted for a left turn, and vice-versa).

After shifting your weight to the opposite (outside) ski, plant the pole on the inside of the turn and lift the inside ski up simultaneously. Quickly bring the inside ski over parallel with the outside ski and complete the turn.

What has happened is easy to see in Figures 94, 95 and 96. As Dennis pushes on the outside ski, he starts to turn in the opposite direction. When he brings the inside ski over and weighs both skis equally, his skis skid through the arc of the turn.

Some things to bear in mind while practicing:

- Since this is a skidded turn, make sure to weight the skis equally the second that inside ski is brought over. Push down on your heels and bend your knees excessively to transmit energy to the tails of your skis. A push on the tails helps the skis skid nicely through the turn.

- Also remember to edge your skis into the slope slightly. If you try this on a flat ski, you will topple downhill or careen out of control across the slope.
- Get used to rotating around your inside pole plant. Plant the pole firmly and come around it to complete the turn.

The best practice for stem christies is to make one turn in one direction, ski up into the contour of the hill to slow down, and then get into the snowplow position before starting a turn in the opposite direction. This exercise should follow practice on left turns and right turns done one at a time.

Parallel

The next building block in our turning program is the parallel turn. Parallel turns, if done properly, are carved rather than skidded. This means the skis are set on edge and then carved through the snow on their sidecamber.

The secret to successful paralleling is weighting and unweighting the skis. Look at Dennis making the turn in Figures 97, 98 and 99. He has bent knees and his hands are out front in the "ready" position. He initiates the turn with a quick shift of weight to his outside ski and plant of his inside pole. Then he rises up, straightening his knees as the weight shift is completed.

The weight shift complete, he brings the inside ski over and drives his knees down as he equalizes his weight on both skis. To complete the turn, he drives his knees even lower and points them slightly into the slope in the direction of the turn. Notice the hands in the "ready" position and how they lead through the turn; very important, those hands!

To get the feeling of a parallel turn, start with your skis in a wide (shoulder width) tracked position. Get into an aggressive crouch with your hands out in the "ready" position. Move down your practice slope and practice the basic moves. As you improve, ski in a more erect position and learn to steer with your hands as you complete the turn.

The Telemark

For the record, the telemark turn was originated by Norwegian ski jumpers many years ago as a way to turn their long cumbersome jumping skis at the end of the jump outrun. Today, jumpers are still judged on the quality of their telemark position when they land. The telemark turn was not invented by cross-country skiers in Colorado or Washington as popular myth would have us believe.

The telemark is a very useful cross-country turn in deep powder or crud snow conditions. It is also a very enjoyable turn to make. In this introduction to the telemark, we'll stick to the turn in its original form. That is a long sweeping turn, not the modern choppy, quasi-parallel version so often seen at ski areas.

There are many ways of teaching the telemark. I like to tell people to start from a snowplow and get to know the body position and turn from this familiar position. Try this exercise while standing stationary on the snow:

- Assume the snowplow position.
- Weight the right ski.
- As you weight the right ski, start flexing your knees downward. Begin to slide the right ski forward and the left ski back.
- Get into the proper telemark position as shown in Figures 100 and 101.

Now check to make sure the right leg is extended forward properly (lead with the knee, not the toe) and that the ski is angled into the direction of the turn. The trailing leg should form a ninety degree angle at the knee. The lower part of the leg is parallel to the snow; the upper part is perpendicular. If you are up too high with the trailing leg, drop the knee closer to the ski. Make sure the trailing ski is edged in toward the binding of the lead ski.

Now check your body position. The upper body should be erect with the weight equalized over both skis. The hands should be low in the "ready" position. Don't hold your arms and hands way out to the side like outriggers.

A note on the hands; most beginning telemarkers lead through their telemark turn with the arm on the same side as the turning or lead leg. Just as in the diagonal stride, keep the opposite arm and leg movement in mind while telemarking. Lead with the arm opposite the lead leg for a sharper, more effective turn.

Now work on making a few stationary moves into the telemark position. Once ready to try moving turns, do this exercise before starting:

- Put your skis in a wide tracked stance and start down the practice hill.
- As you slide along, practice dropping down into the telemark position with one leg ahead. After coming back up, put the other leg ahead as you drop into another telemark position.
- Alternate lead skis as you move down the slope.

After this exercise, try a few turns from the basic snowplow position and then shift over into the straight running position. Try to slip into the telemark position from this stance. Use the stance that allows you to have a better handle on the basics of the telemark turn.

Perhaps the hardest part of learning the telemark is balance. Weight may seem to be either too far forward or too far back. Your upper torso may seem to throw you off balance. The best remedies are to make sure your weight is equalized on the skis and to drop down into a deeper telemark position when you feel unstable (refer to Fig. 102, 103 and 104).

If your skis fail to turn, try pushing more weight onto the lead ski to edge it more sharply. If you turn too sharply, fall back onto your trailing ski and work on weight equalization.

For best results, keep your head up. I realize this is a lot to ask when you're trying a difficult move like the telemark, but keeping your head up and eyes focused on your direction will do wonders in making your telemark smoother.

A final note on the telemark; it's a tough turn to learn and master. It takes a lot of muscle control, so you have to get in shape to do well.

If you plan to ride the ski lifts and telemark all day, pay particular attention to muscular conditioning. In the last part of this book we'll talk about conditioning and exercise that will help your telemarking muscles. Don't believe those who tell you telemarking doesn't require skill or conditioning.

Hockey Stop

Everyone is impressed with one of those fast, skis together, snow flying stops made by a hot cross-country skier. This is the hockey stop, taking its name from the ice-flying stop on skates (refer to Fig. 105).

To execute a hockey stop, start with your skis in a fairly wide tracked stance on a gentle well groomed slope. Get up some speed and decide which direction you wish to face when you stop. If you want to stop facing the right, do the following:

- Plow the left ski ever so slightly to slow you down and begin to change your direction.
- As you weight and plow the left ski, bring the right ski over and parallel as fast as you can.
- Bring the right ski in close to the left ski, edge both, and bend your knees sharply to bring your equalized weight down firmly onto the skis so they skid to a stop. The sharper the bend and angle to the slope with your knees, the better the edging and quicker the stop.

A firm inside pole plant can help to initiate a jump onto the ski for this stop. Be sure your poles are out of the way as you come to a stop. An errant pole on your downhill side could catch the skis, throwing you over in a wicked fall.

FIG. 91: *The sideslipping position.*

FIG. 92: *Sit back and down for best off-track powder downhills.*

FIG. 93: *Set for traversing downhill.*

FIG. 94: *The stem turn*

FIG. 95

FIG. 96

FIG. 97: *The parallel turn.*

FIG. 98

FIG. 99

FIG. 100: *A front view of the proper telemark position.*

FIG. 101: *Side view of the proper telemark position.*

FIG. 102: *A properly executed telemark turn.*

FIG. 103

FIG. 104

FIG. 105: *The flashy snow-spraying hockey stop.*

PART IV

ADVANCED TRACK TECHNIQUE

Introduction

Now we move onto advanced track technique. Our concern is not racing technique, although after mastering some of the techniques we'll talk about, you should feel comfortable entering a citizens' race.

The step up from beginning to advanced track technique is not too big if you started with the proper fundamentals. If, however, you received improper instruction or improvised your own self-teaching method, you may have developed poor skiing habits that will be hard to break.

The secret to advanced technique is keeping movements simple. The flairs, flourishes and hitches picked up as a beginner now have to be eliminated in favor of solid, uncluttered style. Maximum efficiency is your skiing goal—efficiency gained by making each movement count in propelling yourself down the track.

As with the first part of this book, emphasis will be on the kick and glide (diagonal stride) technique. From the kick and glide, we'll move into the double pole, kick double pole, and some ideas on turning.

Demonstrating the various phases of advanced track technique is Paul Daly, the 1982 National Masters Champion at both 30 and 10 kilometers. Paul is a student of cross-country technique which comes to him naturally after years of hard training. He is active in the U.S. Ski Coaches Association and works with many top junior competitors.

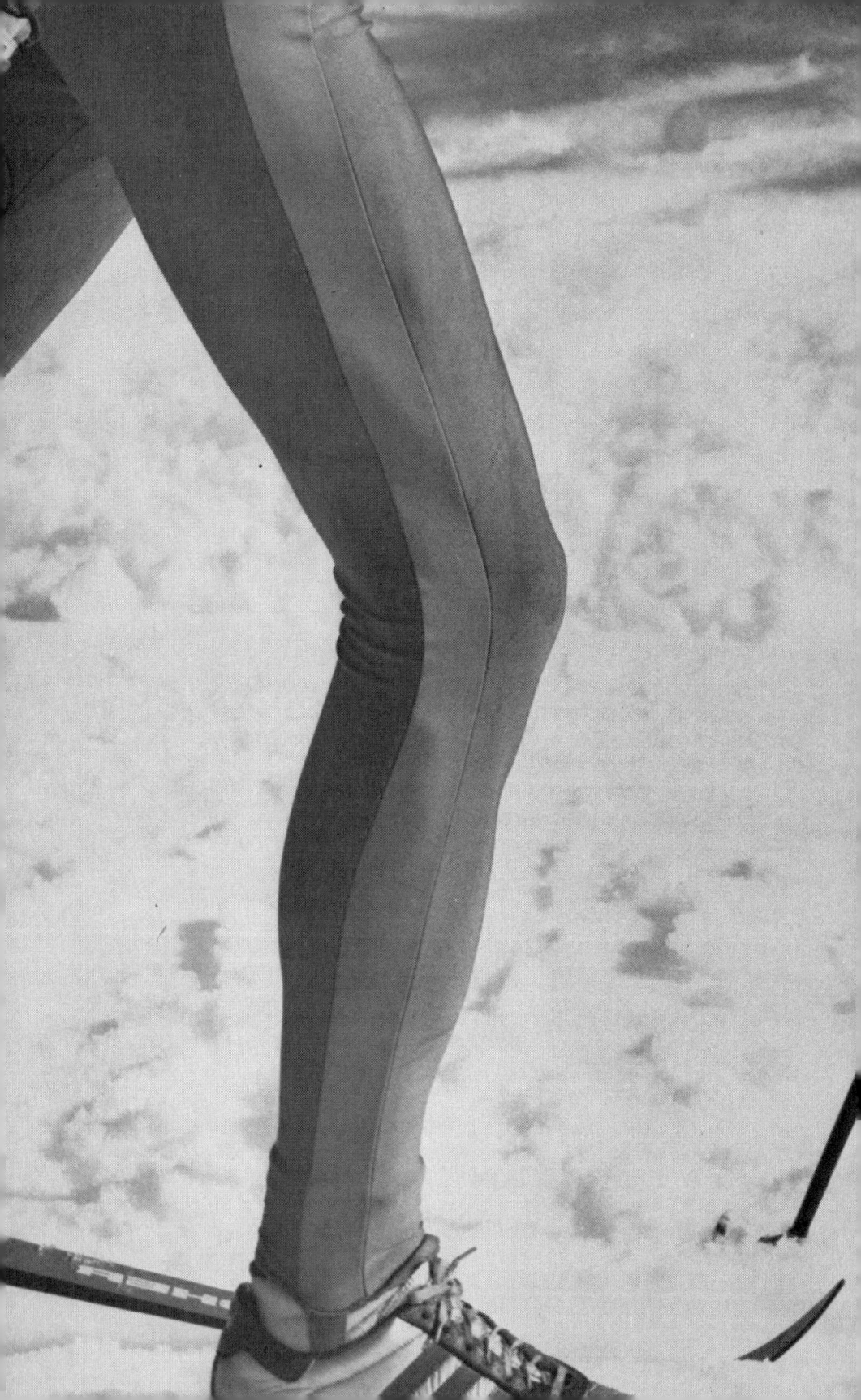

12

FOCUSING ON THE DIAGONAL

Let's start our look at advanced diagonal (kick and glide) technique by checking body position. In Part I, the emphasis was on leg and arm movements for efficient kicking and gliding. Now we add the all-important body positioning elements to complete the picture of the perfect diagonal.

Figures 106, 107, and 108 show Paul assuming right and wrong upper body positions. In the correct position, Paul has these special traits (refer to Fig. 109):

- body arched slightly forward;
- shoulders rolled inward as if he's about to hug a barrel;
- hips tucked under by contracting his abdominal muscles;
- head up and aligned with his trunk;
- eyes looking down the track.

In the incorrect position, Paul bends excessively at the waist and his rear juts out. He also demonstrates a typical fault—sitting back too far on your skis (refer to Fig. 110).

When you try the proper body positioning, the first thing you may notice is the strain on your lower back and abdominal muscles. These strains can be remedied by sit ups and other abdominal conditioning exercises which will be discussed in Part V.

For correct lower body position, tuck the rear under the body by pulling up with the abdominal muscles.

In Figure 111, Paul skis with a slightly bent knee. You may recall that in basic kick and glide technique we stressed bending the knees to get the feel of both the kick and the glide. Now we want to ski with less bend in the knee.

When the kicking leg moves to the rear it should extend naturally as shown in the "right-position," Figure 112. Try to avoid bicycling the leg as shown in the "wrong," Figure 113.

Weight is centered over the ball of the foot during each kick and is evenly distributed on the entire foot during the initial part of the glide (as the kicking ski comes back in). Then it shifts toward the heel as the gliding ski is pushed down the track.

If you sit back too far with your weight on your heels throughout the kick and glide, you will be unable to shift your weight completely from ski to ski.

Arms

The essentials of good arm movement do not change in advanced technique. Let's review some of the key points about arm movement:

- *Natural pendulum motion;* try to eliminate exaggerated forward and backward swings. Swing your arms through an arc with a natural, relaxed motion.
- *Bent arm for power;* on your pole plant, make sure your arm is bent for maximum power. Straight arms equal reduced pole plant power.
- *Release and natural extension;* as you push on the pole for power, release your grip on the pole's handle as it passes your leg. Let the arm extend naturally to the rear. Do not hold onto the pole through an entire poling motion or "throw" your pole away after it passes your leg.

Look at the natural movements Paul demonstrates in the opening sequence shots of this section. They provide a good idea of what the arms should do.

Here are a couple of new arm ideas to consider. First—lead down the track with the forward arm. If you project your lead arm down the track, it will help get your weight up over the skis for better kick and glide. Figure 114 shows what we mean by leading down the track.

Paul's arm comes out to an almost stiff position for a moment before being bent for pole plant power. This forward projection down the track raises him up over his skis and keeps his body angled forward down the track.

Notice in Figure 115 how he bends his arms excessively. We call this "runners" arms; it is the most typical fault skiers have with the diagonal technique. Using arm motions like a runner hinders your down-the-track movement.

Secondly, to help project that leading arm down the track, look at Figure 116 of Paul's hand. By simply angling his wrist slightly forward with his thumb pointing down the track, he helps guide his arm out and down the track before the bent arm pole plant. Think of this when you try the hand adjustment; visualize a string attached to your thumb pulling on it so that it makes your arm extend out and down the track.

Slapping

With some new body positioning and arm movement ideas, you start practicing. A good way to check your diagonal progress is to listen for slapping. Do your skis make a slapping noise as you bring them forward from the extension of your kick?

The slaps mean something is wrong with your diagonal. Chances are you have the wrong body position, incomplete weight transfer, or faulty arm or leg movements that bring the trailing ski down onto the track too soon.

Ideally, the trailing foot/leg should be brought down to the snow alongside the gliding ski and when the feet meet, the skier's weight is shifted onto the trailing leg as it goes into the glide portion of its pendulum movement. Look at the next two Figures. In Figure 117, Paul's leg comes in well behind the other leg. In Figure 118, the feet come together and the transfer of weight begins.

Here are some of the faults that cause slap and their corrections:

- *Sitting back.* If your weight is back on your heels during the diagonal, it is impossible for your trailing leg to swing through in a pendulum-like motion. To correct this fault, try to tuck your rear under your body and arch your upper body slightly forward while centering your weight over the entire foot. You may feel unstable, but you're on the right track.
- *Runner's Arms.* We talked about this briefly. If you have runner's arms, you will be forced into too erect a stance with your weight back on your heels. To correct this, make sure you work on "leading" down the track with your arms. Also consider the subtle movement of your weight on the skis as you ski along. Your weight is over the ball of the foot during the kick, equally distributed along the foot as glide begins, and back towards your heel as the glide is completed. The weight "slides" from the ball of the foot rearward through the kick and glide cycle of one leg. The shift toward the heel is very important in allowing the ski to glide weightless on its forward portion during the glide phases.

- *Leg Pendulum.* We mentioned the bicycling leg. If you bicycle the leg, you bring it up like a cyclist on his upstroke pedalling motion. A bicycled trailing leg is often brought down too quickly and well behind the stationary leg of the gliding ski. To correct this fault, practice swinging one leg back while holding yourself up by your ski poles. Notice how your body feels when the leg is extended naturally. Then bicycle the leg and feel the difference. Try to get the right feeling as you ski. Stop when you think you're slipping back into bicycling, repeat the stationary exercise and strive to get the right feeling locked in your mind.
- *Incomplete weight transfer.* Partial weight transfer invariably results in slaps of the trailing ski. To correct incomplete transfers of weight, think about forward leg drive, not kick. Extend your glide as long as you can by riding your ski. Concentrate on pushing all your weight onto the gliding ski.

In reference to that last tip, keep in mind the following—best technique comes from a natural kick and an emphasized forward leg drive. Too many skiers try to develop flashy horse-like kicks thinking they are the secret of down-the-track power. Unfortunately, most horse kicks result in energy going backwards instead of forwards down the track. Kick down sharply with short rearward movement for a natural kick, then think forward leg drive.

Uphill Diagonal

When you make the decision to become an advanced skier, you open a Pandora's box of technical subtleties. I hope to keep things simple, but bear in mind that these subtleties are important. Some of the more important in advanced technique come in the diagonal technique up gently sloping hills.

In Part I, we looked at the Latin dance, uphill shuffling technique. The dance shuffle introduces you to the faster tempo of the uphill diagonal.

In advanced technique, changing gears is most important in making your uphill diagonal work. You must anticipate an upcoming hill and just before the transition at the base of the hill, shift from a smooth rhythmic kick and glide into a faster tempo with more emphasis on strong, short poling movements and faster kicks and glides.

Your basic body position remains unchanged from the technique on the flats (too much forward lean will throw you onto your face), but the skis and hands move more quickly.

The shortened uphill diagonal kick helps ensure a solid grip on the snow for a fraction of a second. After the quick, aggressive kick, let the ski extend naturally. The rearward extension will be short (refer to Fig. 119, 120 and 121).

When you bring the trailing ski forward, drive the leg forward. As you weight the gliding ski, push the ski forward while your weight comes back to be centered over your heel. Try not to sit back or drop your hips down. With your hands held low, extend your arms up the hill as far as possible without pulling you off balance. Put more pressure on the poles before releasing them.

All too often the hills seem a little slicker than the rest of the track. It takes added technique to press your skis down for grip. Look at the photos and notice how the skier's body weight has been compressed down simply by bending his knees more. He hasn't dropped his rear down; he lowered his center of gravity by compressing his knees. This puts more weight onto the skis for better grip.

In the first picture of the sequence Paul is midway between a kick and glide. The left foot will come in alongside the right prior to the weight shift. Notice the low hands.

Too often beginning skiers misinterpret a better skier's uphill diagonal. They see the skier running up the hill instead of skiing up the hill. In fact the better skier is skiing up, keeping his skis in contact with the snow in a faster diagonal stride.

Running, or bounding, uphill is not only tiring but inefficient, and can bring about wax problems. If you bound or run, your body works much harder than when kicking and gliding. Hills are hard enough without adding work.

Considering the wax problem, has this ever happened to you? You get tired of trying to diagonal up the hill, so you run a few yards lifting your skis up out of the snow. After a few steps, you begin to notice your skis collecting a layer of snow underfoot. A few steps more and you have a foot-deep platform of snow underfoot. I call skis in this condition "pimp skis" after the famous, high-heeled platform shoes worn by the gentlemen of such dubious distinction.

This is normally caused by moisture in the air creating a thin layer of ice on your wax as you lift your skis out of contact with the snow. The ice attracts loose snow and soon you're balled-up underfoot. The only solution now is getting a scraper out and removing the platform. You can avoid the whole problem by keeping your skis in contact with the snow in a steady uphill diagonal.

Double Poling

The secret to advanced double poling is refinement. To make the step up to advanced skiing, you have to streamline your double pole technique. Check the following (refer to Fig. 122, 123 and 124).

- As you rise up onto the double pole position, make sure your arms are bent slightly and the poles are angled slightly backward.
- Think of letting your entire body weight fall onto your poles as you begin your push through.
- Push with your arms and shoulder girdle muscles.
- Push through and release the poles as they pass your legs. Don't flair or throw the poles away on their backswing.
- Check your body movement. It's bend at the waist and drop the upper torso, not sit down and flex your knees.

Kick Double Pole

Skiers have more problems with the kick double pole than any other cross-country technique. It takes time and concentration to make this movement smooth and effortless.

The only thing we can add to Part I is how to most effectively use this technique while skiing. It is the best maneuver for skiing off the top of a hill. A quick kick double pole will provide the thrust needed to gain speed for a following downhill or flat.

Take a look at Paul making a kick double pole at the top of a short rise in Figure 125. He makes his kick just at the apex of the hill before the downward transition begins. Try to do the same at the top of each hill you ski. You'll be amazed how much energy and forward momentum one kick double pole will give you.

The other occasion where the kick double pole works perfectly is when you're skiing along a section of flat or gently sloping track where the diagonal stride and double pole don't work. You'll begin to notice sections of track like this as you ski more. You attempt to diagonal along but you're moving too fast to get a smooth diagonal going. On the other hand, your speed isn't great enough to get a fast double pole going. The answer to your dilemma, kick double poling. A section of track that is best double poled when snow conditions are fast will most likely be best kick double poled when snow conditions are slow. A slow diagonal stride section (slightly inclined up) may be kick double poled when snow conditions are faster than normal.

Faster In-Track Turns

Again, as with the kick double-pole, we have already mastered the basics necessary for faster in-track turns. All you have to do is practice fast skates and steps to make it all perfect. Remember to keep the body low with the hands out in the "ready" position for best step and skate results.

There is another turn, the parallel turn, that is very effective on well prepared track systems where groomers blank, or wash out, high speed corners. Eradicating the tracks in a fast corner allows the skier to select his/her line into the turn and use any turn, from snowplow to parallel, to get through safely.

The snowplow is the safest turn through a fast corner. Often however, an aggressive skate, or a series of short, quick step turns will do the job nicely. But these all have to be done at moderate speed. So when you're moving fast, rely on the parallel turn to get you through the corner without losing too much speed (refer to Fig. 126).

The best way to parallel through a fast corner is:

- Weight the ski on the outside of the turn just slightly as you approach the corner.
- As you enter the corner, quickly shift your weight to the outside ski and bring the inside ski alongside.
- Weight the skis equally and press down on your heels.
- Be sure to keep a low body position and your hands out in the "ready" position.

Riding The Corners

If the tracks remain around a corner, try the following to ride through without tumbling:

- As you approach the corner, compress your knees to drop your body weight down. At the same time, get your hands down into the "ready" position (refer to Fig. 127).
- As you go into the corner, weight the inside ski and lean slightly toward the inside of the turn. The physical force of turning tends to throw you to the outside of the corner. Your weighted inside ski and slight lean will help overcome the thrust to the outside.
- If you get out of control, drop down closer to your skis and place your hands out to the side so your arms become stabilizing outriggers.

Something Special

I mentioned in the introduction that our Yankee ingenuity had helped change the face of cross-country instruction. In addition, certain American skiers have helped change the face of advanced technique. No one has had more influence on international racing technique than Vermonter Bill Koch, certainly the greatest American cross-country competitor.

Bill began working a few years ago on a new flat terrain technique to replace the double pole. The technique was designed for long marathon races where hours of diagonalling can be inefficient and boring. The technique he devised could also be used to supplant the kick double pole and double pole when necessary. The technique became known as the "marathon skate."

The "marathon skate" is simply putting one ski out of the track and skating with it while the other ski remains in the track. With each skate the skier double poles. Paul demonstrates the "marathon skate" on the flats and then shows how you come around a corner with it in Figures 128 and 129. Notice on the corner, he skates with his outside ski.

During a 1982 season, Koch's racing success led most of the top international racers to start using the marathon skate. But not the Norwegians; their head coach scoffed, saying the "marathon skate" was inefficient and would keep Koch from winning a World Championship medal. Continuing with this technique, Koch won a World Championship medal and the overall World Cup title.

Try the "marathon skate," and add it to your repertoire of cross-country technique. It may well replace some of the traditional advanced techniques in future years.

FIG. 106

FIG. 107

FIG. 108

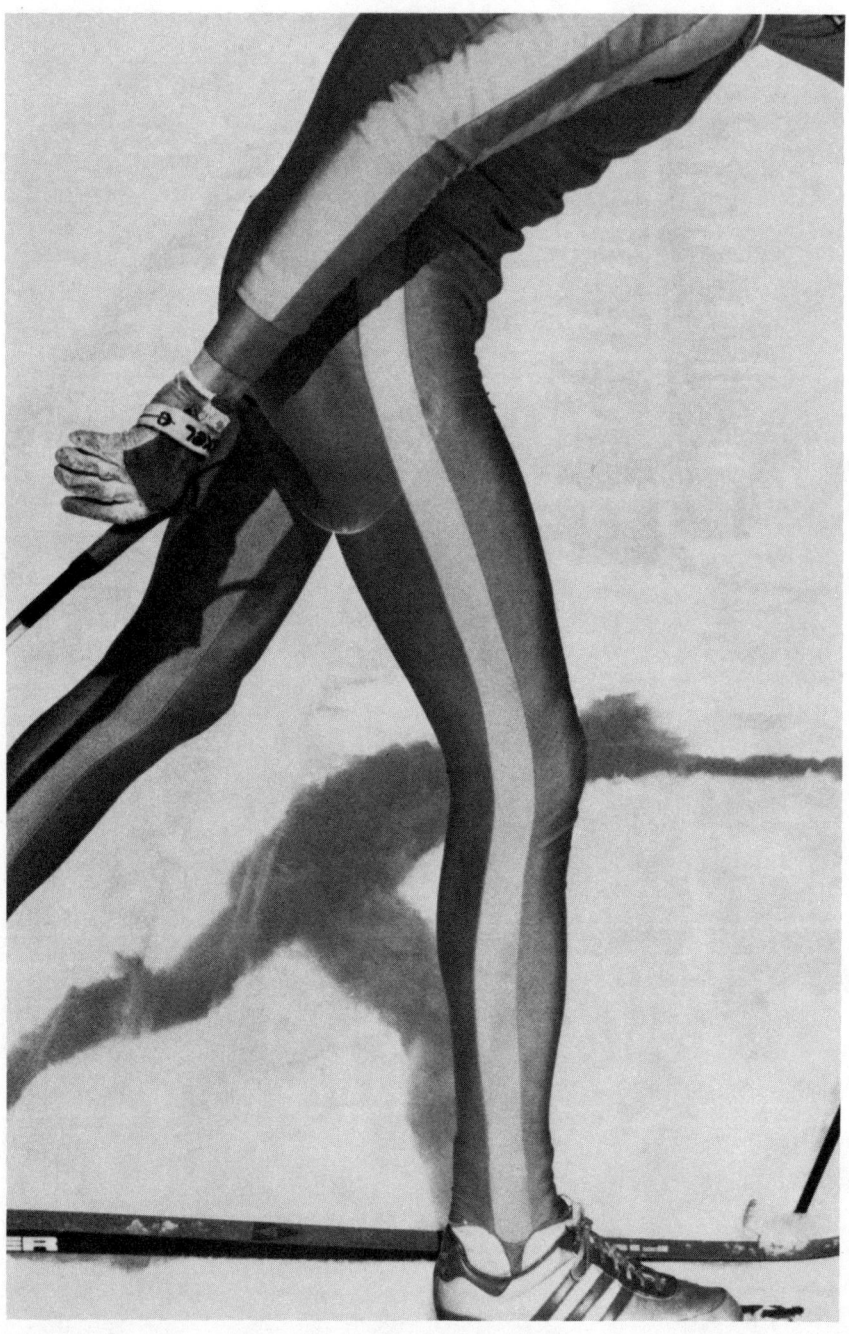

FIG. 109: *The right body position.*

FIG. 110: *Wrong—keep your rear in.*

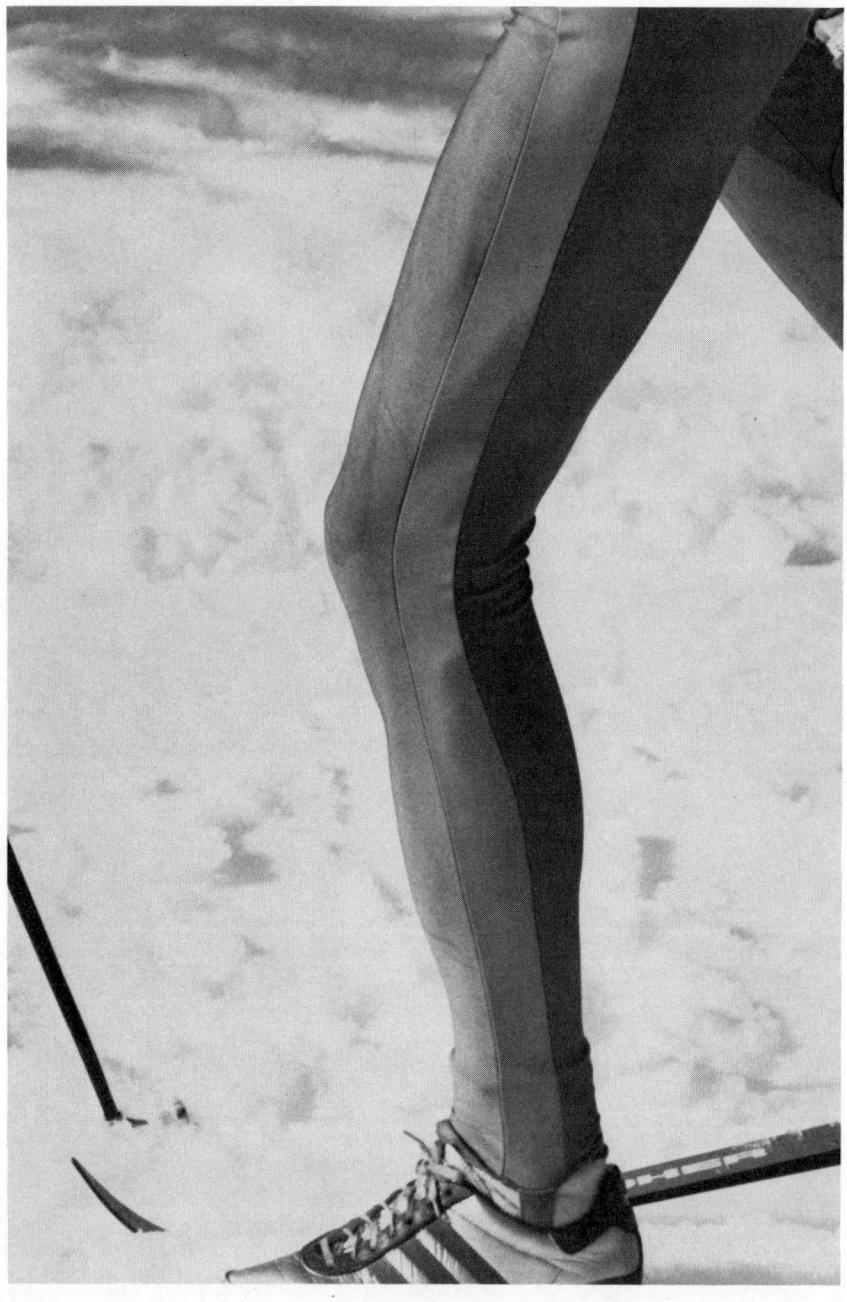

FIG. 111: *The proper leg positioning—slightly bent knee—straight shin.*

FIG. 112: *The "right" naturally trailing leg.*

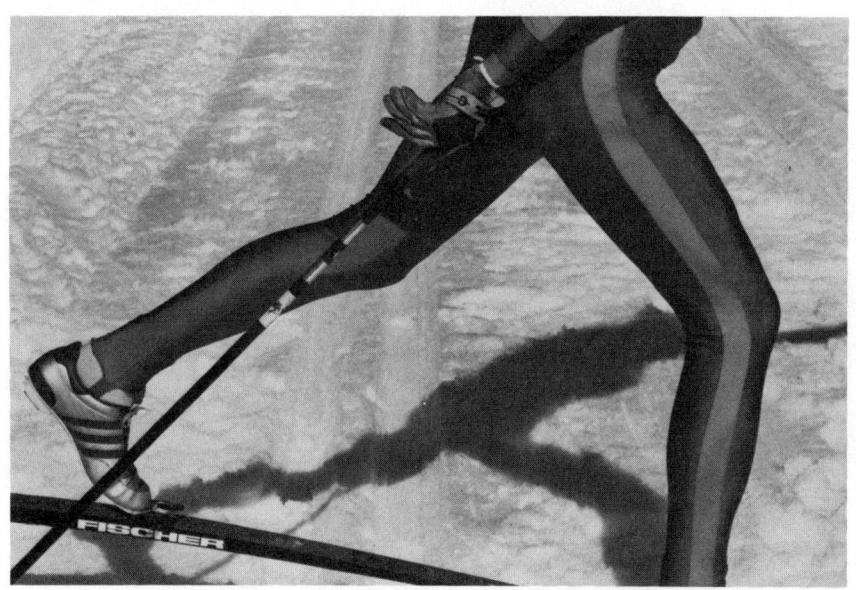

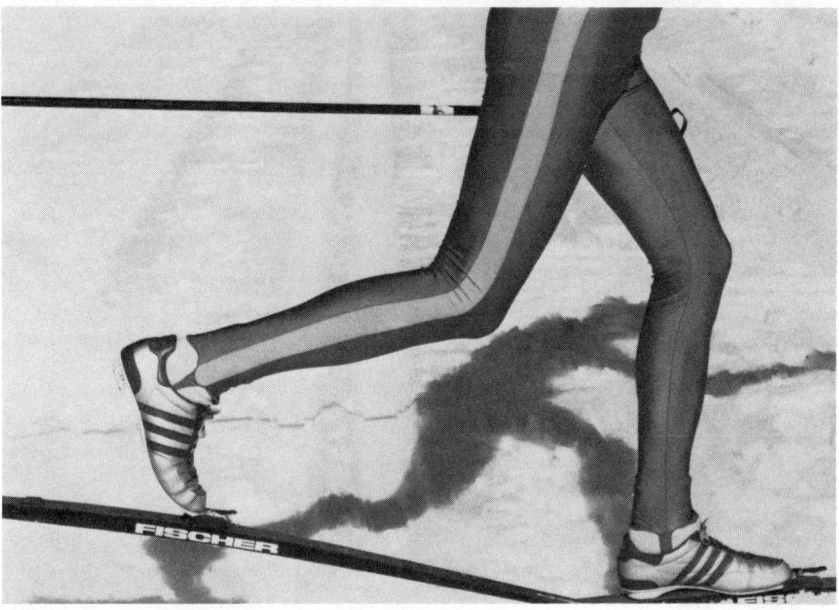

FIG. 113: *"Bicycling the leg."*

FIG. 114: *Leading down the track with your arms.*

FIG. 115: *A typical problem—"runners" arms.*

FIG. 116: *Angle the wrist to help lead your arm down the track.*

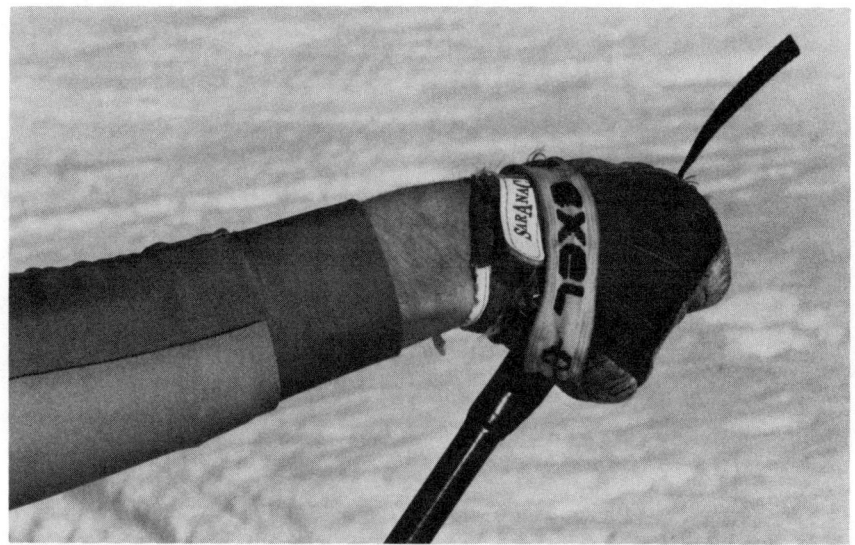

FIG. 117: *What happens when you hear that slapping noise on your diagonal.*

FIG. 118: *How your legs should come together during the diagonal.*

FIG. 119: *The uphill diagonal.*

FIG. 120

FIG. 121

FIG. 122: Advanced double poling. Check that second figure. Notice Paul is getting down with some power.

FIG. 123

FIG. 124

FIG. 125: *Kick double pole off the top of a short rise.*

FIG. 126: *Hold on during those fast parallel turns.*

FIG. 127: *Proper positioning for riding the fast tracked corners.*

FIG. 128: *The marathon skate technique.*

FIG. 129: *Marathon skating a corner.*

PART V

CONDITIONING

Introduction

Practice makes perfect. This old adage is not quite true when it comes to cross-country skiing. Granted, the more time you spend on skis, the better skier you'll become. But there is another important ingredient in any successful skier's program—conditioning. You can work for years on technique, but if you don't prepare yourself physically for the tasks at hand, your work will go for naught.

Far too many cross-country skiers look on conditioning as something for racers. They feel they can get by with minimal pre-season conditioning programs or "ski themselves into shape." Both ideas are wrong. You have to set out a conditioning program and follow it over a period of months to arrive on snow ready to go.

While I don't suggest you try the type of strict programs followed by top athletes, I do suggest you try to get into a modicum of shape. Being in shape will make each day of cross-country skiing less tiring and more enjoyable. The time spent on conditioning will also pay dividends in your normal daily life. Consider conditioning carefully.

A basic conditioning program should be varied and enjoyable. It should focus on cardiovascular conditioning to increase the strength of your heart and lungs. Overall muscular development should be given equal time. And you should find enjoyable outdoor sports that test your cardiovascular and muscular abilities off-season.

13

CARDIOVASCULAR TRAINING

The cardiovascular system (heart and lungs) is the engine that runs our bodies. The muscles and joints are the gears and levers. The first responsibility of a person seeking to get his or her body ready for the rigors of cross-country skiing is cardiovascular development.

There are many ways to develop a healthy heart and lungs. Jogging naturally comes to mind. Bicycling, stationary cycling, swimming and hiking are also first rate activities. With any of these exercises, consistency is important. You should try to put in fifteen to twenty minutes per day, five days a week to gain any conditioning benefits.

If you plan to ski more aggressively and train for a tour race, increase your conditioning period to a half-hour per day. The benefits of consistent cardiovascular training combined with a proper diet will be increased endurance and loss of weight, a nice combination for any skier.

A note of warning before you start out on a cardiovascular strengthening program; check with your physician if you have not been active for several years. Let your personal physician set limitations for your initial training period.

Jogging/Running

Any jogging program should start out slowly and build up as the jogger becomes adjusted to the exercise and the muscular aches and pains that often accompany the increase in activity.

If you are totally out of shape, it may take up to five months to get to a point where jogging will make an appreciable impact on your cross-country skiing. Once a base of conditioning has been established, try to take your runs over mixed terrain. This means equal amounts of flat, uphill and downhill running, similar to what you'd find on a typical ski trail.

As a rule of thumb, run at a steady pace on the flats, push a little harder on the uphills, and relax (slow down) to minimize the pounding effect on the downhills. The intervals of different pacing make your heart work harder. The heart rests on the downhill, then pushes up a few beats on the flats before making a big jump in beats per minute to get the jogger up that hill. Such interval training over mixed terrain is essential for good cardiovascular conditioning.

Swimming

Swimming is an excellent alternative to jogging. Many people substitute swimming for jogging because they hate the aches and pains of the latter. World marathon record holder Alberto Salazar took up swimming when his running injuries curtailed his training. He swam while he healed and it worked. A few months later he was back on the roads and won his first New York Marathon.

The problem with swimming for most people is they cheat a bit. They get wet; breast stroke a lap; rest, and a few minutes later swim another lap. This isn't doing a thing for your body or cardiovascular system.

Select a stroke (freestyle) and swim several laps before resting. Try to build your swimming up to a point where you can sustain a stroke over a period of time. Rest between longer sustained swims for positive swimming results. Swimming works the upper body and lower body muscle groups and is just as beneficial as jogging for the cardiovascular system.

Bicycling

What if you hate jogging and despise the over-chlorination of your local swimming pool? Try bicycling. To me, bicycling for conditioning means everything from riding your balloon-tired klunker to the grocery, to higher speed tours on ten-speeds. No matter what you ride, time spent on your bicycle will give you many cardiovascular rewards.

Normally it takes about twice as much time on a bicycle to get the same conditioning benefit that you would from jogging or swimming. Try to keep your rides over mixed terrain. Ride along at a moderate pace on the flats, increase your tempo some on the uphills, and rest on the downs.

Be careful about your knees when cycling. By this I mean you shouldn't push too much in high gears. Most cyclists feel that if they aren't pushing against a great deal of resistance, they aren't making progress. Top cyclists prefer to "spin" as they ride, using lower gears and moving their legs faster. Spinning is easier on the knees and just as effective as pounding against high gears.

Stationary Bicycling

Housebound on a bleak rainy day, I sit astride a stationary bicycle and get a workout while I watch the news on television. Stationary bicycles are good cardiovascular training devices if used properly. Unfortunately, too many people use them without gaining any conditioning effect.

To get the most from a stationary cycle ride, vary the resistance against which you pedal. Start off with little resistance to warm up. After spinning for a period of time, increase the resistance load for a short period. Alternate the resistance loads throughout your timed workout. A note of caution; do not push against too much resistance. This will help prevent knee injuries.

Walking/Hiking

Top athletes may scoff, but walking can be as beneficial to your cardiovascular system as jogging. That is, providing you walk at a moderate pace for a set period of time. Working at the lower heart rates produced in walking has been proven to be most effective in burning fat. If you want to shed a few pounds easily, watch your diet and take up walking.

Hiking is just as beneficial. Moreover, it has the extra dimension of a more natural setting and, hopefully, clean air. As with walking, hike for a set time without long rest periods between stages of the hike.

Hill Walking with Poles

For people who would like to get the most from a conditioning workout, I suggest *hill walking* with poles. The walking works on your cardiovascular system; the poling motions work your arms, shoulder girdle and upper back muscles. This is total body conditioning (refer to Fig. 130).

For best results with this exercise, find a gentle uphill for practice. Stride out up the hill, planting your uphill pole firmly as you move. Push on the pole as you step up and release it from your grip as it passes your leg (refer to Fig. 131).

Fifteen minutes of hill walking with poles is plenty for most skiers.

This is a particularly good exercise to work on in the late fall as the ski season approaches.

A more vigorous variation of hill walking with poles is *ski striding with poles* (refer to Fig. 132). You push up the hill vigorously on each stride going at a faster tempo. Push off the rear foot, and as it leaves the ground, reach as far forward up the hill as possible with your lead pole. Each pole plant is vigorous. Ski striding is recommended for those in better shape who are looking for a harder workout.

Still another variation of hill walking with poles is *hiking with poles*. Stride alone easily on the flats and uphills and use your poles for balancing and assistance on downhills.

Conditioning Indicator

One of the best indicators of how your cardiovascular conditioning is progressing is your pulse. Learning to take your pulse from your wrist, or carotid artery in your neck, is an important part of conditioning. Count the pulse beats for six seconds and then multiply by ten to get the pulse rate.

To understand this pulse rate and how it affects conditioning, you must first establish a set of personal pulse criteria. Here is how you establish these criteria:

- Upon awakening some morning, take your pulse while still a bit groggy. This is your resting rate.
- Next, subtract your age from 200 if you are male, and 225 if you are a female. These are the maximum heart rates established for males and females. The rate achieved by subtracting your age from the maximum rate equals your personal maximum rate.
- You can now calculate your training rate by using this formula: Personal maximum rate minus (−) resting pulse, times (×) 65%, plus (+) resting pulse = training rate.

During exercise, when you get above the number of beats indicated by the formula as your training rate, you are beginning to realize the conditioning effect. To monitor your performance while exercising, stop every so often and take your pulse. If you're not up to your training rate, step up your activity.

Do not go as hard as possible, working at your maximum heart rate, for as long as you can. Red-lining your heart like a car's engine is dangerous. Set an upper limit of say 165 or 170 beats per minute and try to stay below that rate during conditioning.

Now, to make sure you have the whole pulse picture, let's use a typical cross-country skier and see what his training rate should be. John Typical is 35 years old and has a resting pulse rate of 50.

Subtracting his age from the maximum male rate, we find John's personal maximum rate to be 165 beats per minute.

Now let's put John's numbers into the formula to see what his basic conditioning pulse rate will be:

165 (personal maximum rate) −50 (resting pulse) = 105

105 x 65% = 68 + 50 (resting pulse) = *138 beats per minute.*

For best results from his cardiovascular conditioning program, John Typical should keep his pulse rate above 138 beats per minute, but below 165 beats per minute (his maximum heart rate).

FIG. 130

FIG. 131: *Hill walking with poles.*

FIG. 132: *Ski striding with poles—more explosive action.*

14

CONDITIONING MUSCLE GROUPS

One thing is certain about cross-country skiing; it works practically every muscle group in your body. With the exception of hill walking with poles and swimming, the cardiovascular exercises just discussed focus on the lower body activity. To be truly prepared for a season of cross-country skiing, you have to strengthen your upper body as well.

This may be accomplished through a good weight training program designed for you by a professional at one of your local, reputable health clubs. If this type of workout has never appealed to you, try a circuit course consisting of several exercise stations. You jog from station to station, exercising different muscle groups that will often come into play during skiing.

Outdoors, I set up a circuit course in the woods. During winter, or whenever the weather is poor, I set up a circuit course indoors. Rather than jog between stations indoors, I insert a stationary bicycle ride, or running in-place, between sets of exercise.

The object of the circuit course workout is to build muscle tone, not muscle bulk. For cross-country skiing, you need elastic muscles for endurance more than you need big, bulky muscles for strength. Toning your muscles with exercises on a circuit course prepares them for hours of use on a typical day of skiing.

In the following photographs, my friend Marilyn Bellwood-Mathews helps demonstrate a typical circuit course. A fine runner, Marilyn has become an avid cross-country skier. Like other runners who have taken up cross-country skiing, she found her cardiovascular system and legs up to the task, but her upper body strength lacking. Running, particularly long distance like Marilyn enjoys, does not place any emphasis on upper body strength. But you must have fit upper body muscles for cross-country skiing.

Using whatever natural props were at hand, Marilyn and I set up a circuit course in the woods not far from our respective homes at Klister Corner. We spread the exercise stations over several acres of land so we can jog between stations to get a cardiovascular workout as well as a muscular workout. Here's a look at each exercise station:

- *Dips:* using a fallen log, Marilyn does arm dips (refer to Fig. 133). These are good for strengthening the backs of your arms and shoulders. Be sure to extend out, digging your heels into the ground as Marilyn does. Dip down until your rear almost touches the ground, and come back up until your arms are rigid.
- Hill walk with poles to the next station.
- *Double poling on arm bands:* this is a very specific exercise that helps tone the arm and back muscles. Arm bands are two bicycle inner tubes (27x1¼ inch) tied together after both valve stems have been cut out. Joined together, the two strands form one long tube which can be wrapped around a tree trunk, draped over a tree limb, or wedged between two rocks. Place the arm bands high over head so you pull down on the ends. Wrap your hands around the loose ends and back off until you feel tension in the tubes. Now pull on the tubes until you begin to feel a burning sensation in your muscles (refer to Fig. 134).
- With poles in hand, jog off to the next station (refer to Fig. 135).
- *Single pole exercises:* again using arm bands, practice your kick and glide poling motions. Back off on the tubes to get tension and pull until your arms feel the burning sensation (refer to Fig. 136).
- Jog with poles to the next station.
- *Push-ups off rocks:* good for building up your shoulders and arm muscles (refer to Fig. 137).
- Jog back to the start of the course.

This, then, is a complete circuit course. I do the course several times for a workout. Fellow skiers from Klister Corner generally find one or two circuits sufficient. Total time for completing one circuit is fifteen minutes.

For my indoor circuit, I do the same exercises with these adaptations:

- *Dips:* off the side of the bed, or bench, or between two chairs placed shoulder width apart.

FIG. 133: *Station #1—dips.*

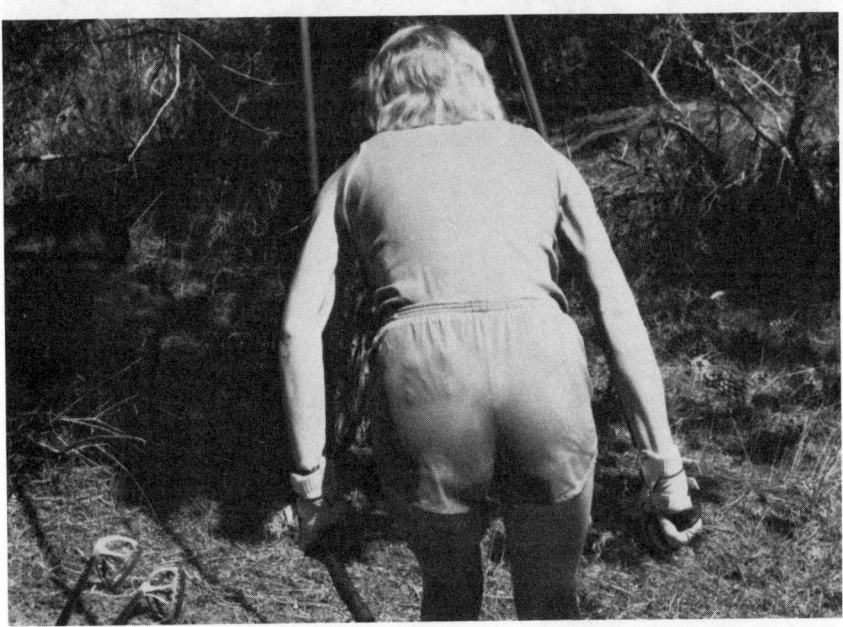

FIG. 134: *Station #2—double poling exercise on arm bands.*

FIG. 135: *Jog between stations with your poles in hand.*

FIG. 136: *Station #3—single pole exercise with arm bands.*

FIG. 137: *Station #4—pushups.*

- *Pushups:* done with my legs (or from waist down) resting on the bed, hands on the floor.
- *Poling:* rather than do both double and single pole exercise with arm bands, I do longer single pole workouts with either an *Exer Genie* or the *Exel 10-190* exercise device. Both devices work on resistance and can be adjusted for light or heavy loads depending upon your mood or muscular conditioning. In the lead photo of Part V Marilyn pulls on the Exer 10-190 set up outside. Indoors, lay the webbing on top of an open door, close the door and the tab at the end of the webbing will keep the device securely in place.
- *Jogging:* substitute stationary cycling or running in-place, or if you are so inclined put on some music and do dance aerobics to get your heart rate up.

On the Road

When I travel, I take along my *Exel 10-190* to try and stay in shape. Every morning before breakfast, I pull on the "10-190" for a few minutes, do some pushups, dips, and run in-place. You begin to lose muscle tone almost immediately, so try and keep in shape with a ten to fifteen minute hotel room routine while you're on the road.

One for the Back

Every sport has a particularly stressful relationship with a part of the human anatomy. Tennis elbow, football knees, and runner's feet immediately come to mind. Cross-country skiing is not different. It effects the lower back more than any part of the body (refer to Fig. 138).

Lower back pain is not uncommon among skiers of all abilities. It can be curbed with a program of regular exercise. Situps are important because they strengthen the abdominal muscles that help support your upper torso. In conjunction with a regular program of situps, you should also be doing back lifts. Marilyn demonstrates this in the next photograph.

With her body off the edge of the table, she clasps her hands behind her head (elbows flared out), then slowly drops down until her body is perpendicular to the floor. Rising back up slowly, she goes to a point where she is parallel with the floor, and in line with the table top.

Two important aspects of this exercise; be sure your waist is at the table's edge to gain the maximum effect of the lifts, and go slowly, never rising above the horizontal plane. Exaggerated movements, or lifts, above the horizontal plane could result in back injury instead of back strengthening.

Marilyn's legs are being held by someone in these photos. Ask a friend to help you with this exercise, or lock your legs under a bench. Some Universal Gyms have a station where you can perform back lifts.

Cross-Country Downhill Exercises

If cross-country downhill skiing captures your fancy, you should prepare for days of making those turns with exercise above and beyond the normal conditioning routine.

First and foremost, work on strengthening your thighs. In cross-country downhill skiing, the thighs (quadriceps and hamstrings) work over-time. They support your upper body weight and help alleviate excessive pressure on your knees. You can strengthen your thighs in two ways; leg extensions on a Universal Gym, and "wall sitters" (refer to Fig. 139).

At home during your circuit course, try the "wall sitter" as shown. Assume the sitting position with your back flat against the wall. Make sure your thighs are carrying the bulk of your upper body weight. (You'll know they are when they begin to quake and get that burning sensation.) Sit until you feel you can't take it any longer, rise up, rest, and return to the sitting position. Repeat for five minutes.

On the Universal Gym, do the exercise as shown in Figure 140, but do not load the exercise device with the most weight you can possibly lift. For best, and safest, exercise, load the device with reasonable weight, and slowly move in and out of the fully extended leg position. Repeat the exercise until your legs send a flash to the brain, "Stop this nonsense, I need a rest." Rest, and repeat.

Compatible Sports

For many of us, the actual work of training, if confined to home or gym, is a drag. But training can be fun, and conditioning need not be a tiresome activity as seen in Figure 141. That's why I recommend using sports like canoeing, kayaking, and backpacking as substitutes for indoor or structured conditioning.

All these fun, outdoor sports have positive cross-over values. The activities in each of the sports will enhance your physical conditioning (cardiovascular and muscular) for cross-country skiing. Backpacking works the cardiovascular system, and what better muscular conditioning than load carrying? Whitewater, flat water, and ocean touring make kayaking a versatile and exciting sport. All forms of kayaking are great for lower back strengthening and upper body toning.

Canoeing has many redeeming features. One of the best, aside from the exercise value, is it can be done with a partner. Sure, you

FIG. 138: *One for the back.*

FIG. 139: *Wall sitters for stronger thighs.*

FIG. 140: *Using the Universal Gym to strengthen the thighs.*

FIG. 141: *Use fun, compatible sports to get ready for a season of skiing.*

can hike or backpack with a partner and kayak with a friend, but there's nothing quite like the teamwork involved in handling a canoe properly. If you like teamwork, try canoeing.

I'm somewhat of a recluse so I like solo canoeing. This is a relatively new form of canoeing. Until recently, there have not been that many special canoes built for the soloist. In the past, if you wanted to solo you had to pilot a big two-person canoe around. Now there are many shorter, quicker, more maneuverable solo canoes on the market.

Paddling one of the sleek solos require some skill and general muscular fitness. You can get your pulse rate up to training level while cruising along the backwaters, or out onto a large lake.

Harry Roberts of Sawyer Canoe claims that within a few weeks of beginning paddling in a solo, you'll be able to paddle for up to an hour at a continuous pulse rate of 130 to 140 beats per minute. As Harry puts it, "Not bad; you can maintain or improve your aerobic fitness, increase strength and tone your skeletal muscles, and have fun doing it."

Scheduling Your Conditioning

I'd never recommend setting too rigid a conditioning schedule. Try to get in five days of exercise per week and vary your activities according to the weather. Start your cardiovascular conditioning well before the start of the ski season (six months if you want to increase performance, four months if you want to get into basic shape).

In the fall, start working on your circuit course program and do more hill walking with poles to get more specific conditioning just before the season starts. Throughout your training/conditioning program use a variety of sports to break up your routine. Canoe, kayak, and backpack spring through "Indian summer." On a nice fall day, get out and enjoy it.

Diet

It goes without saying that a good diet is important to any athlete in training. Too often, diet is overlooked by the average person starting on a basic conditioning program. Diet is probably more important for the neophyte than the top athlete. Watching what and how much you eat can positively affect your endurance and weight loss plans, as well as your mental alertness.

Without delving into the mysteries of nutrition, a task for which I am not fully qualified, let me recite some basic precepts that have worked for many who maintain a healthful outlook on life:

- Avoid junk food.
- Cut down on red meat consumption.
- Avoid overeating, and salt, sugar, and fats.

- Increase your intake of carbohydrates (carbohydrates are your muscles' basic fuel).
- Eat as you feel the need to refuel. Several healthy snacks throughout the day are better than the three "eat-all-you-can" meal-per-day ritual set down by a preceding, portlier, heart attack-prone generation.

To get a better fix on the best diet for you, consult a qualified dietitian or sports physician.

For up-to-date reading on diet and fitness, I suggest Covert Bailey's book, *Fit or Fat,* a best seller that contains enough good information to get you on the right dietary path for better health, athletic endurance and weight loss.

Stretching

Top athletes long ago realized that slow stretching is important before any event. Stretching limbers up the muscles, allowing them time to get ready for vigorous activity.

There are numerous stretching exercises that can be done before a run or a home exercise program. These exercises are best learned from other runners, running magazines, or through an exercise program at the "Y" or community health club. What is important to this book are on-snow stretches performed before each day of skiing starts.

Pictured are five warmup stretches that should be done religiously before each outing:

- *Touch Your Toes:* drop down slowly and hold the "down" position for as long as you can before rising up slowly. Do not bounce in and out of the position; bouncing rapidly can tear a cold muscle. Work slowly and deliberately (refer to Fig 142).
- *Leg Swings:* with your poles on and out for stability, stand on one leg and slowly swing the opposite leg to and fro. Alternate legs (refer to Fig. 143 and 144).
- *Deep Splits:* to stretch the groin muscles, drop slowly into a deep split. Hold the deep position for a few seconds, then rise back up using your arms for power and poles for balance (refer to Fig. 145).
- *Back Poles:* to limber your shoulders and upper back muscles, grasp your poles in front as shown. With almost rigid arms, bring the poles up over your head and down along your back as far as possible. Repeat the complete exercise several times (refer to Fig. 146).
- *Side Bends:* with your arms over your head and hands clasped together, bend side to side slowly. Keep your feet spread wide (refer to Fig. 147).

FIG. 142: *Toe touches—drop down slowly and hold the position.*

FIG. 143: *Leg swings to loosen up.*

FIG. 144

FIG. 145: *Deep splits stretch the groin and lower back muscles.*

FIG. 146: *Back poles.*

FIG. 147: *Side bends—a must before starting out.*

PART VI

SUGGESTED READINGS

Conditioning

- Anderson, Bob. *Stretching.* Shelter Publications, P.O. Box 279, Bolinas, CA 94924; 1980.
  The text on pre and post exercise stretching with a section on cross-country ski stretches.

- Woodward, Bob. *Cross-Country Ski Conditioning for Exercise Skiers and Citizen Racers.* Contemporary Books, Inc., 180 North Michigan Avenue, Chicago, IL 60601; 1981.
  The low key approach to training for skiers of all abilities.

Off-Track Skiing

- Bein, Vic. *Mountain Skiing.* The Mountaineers, 715 Pike Street, Seattle, WA 98101; 1982.
  Going off-track for some serious mountain skiing? Read this book first.

- Watters, Ron. *Ski Camping.* Chronicle Books, 870 Market Street, San Francisco, CA 94102; 1979.
  An excellent primer for ski backpacking trips. Well illustrated.

Racing

- Caldwell, John. *Caldwell on Competitive Cross-Country.* Stephen Green Press, Brattleboro, VT 05301; 1979.
  A realistic approach to racing from one of the sport's finest students, who also happens to make the best maple syrup in Vermont.

- Skag, Halder and Larsson, Olle. *World Cup Cross-Country Technique.* Poudre Press, Box 181, Laport, CO 80535; 1982.
  Unsurpassed in presentation of cross-country racing techniques through sequence photos. For those who seek the best form.

General

- Bailey, Covert. *Fit or Fat.* Houghton Mifflin Company, 2 Park Street, Boston, Mass. 02107; 1978.
  A best seller that puts exercise and weight loss into sharp focus. A must for the overweight.

- *Canoe Aerobics.* Sawyer Canoe, Box 435, Oscoda, MI 48750.
  Free of charge. A pamphlet that gives some insight into how canoeing can be a valuable form of fun exercise.